Japonisme

Thorsons
An imprint of
HarperCollins*Publishers*
1 London Bridge Street
London SE1 9GF

www.harpercollins.co.uk

First published by
HarperCollins*Publishers* 2018

9 10 8

A catalogue record of this book is
available from the British Library

ISBN 978-0-00-828604-0

Printed and bound in Latvia

MIX
Paper from
responsible sources
FSC™ C007454

This book is produced from
independently certified FSC paper to
ensure responsible forest management.
For more information visit:
www.harpercollins.co.uk/green

Japonisme

Ikigai, forest bathing, wabi-sabi and more

Erin Niimi Longhurst
新美英鈴

Illustrations by Ryo Takemasa 武政諒

Contents

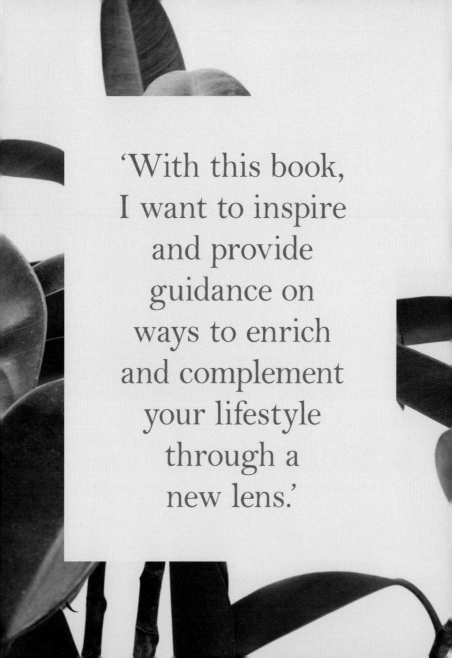

'With this book, I want to inspire and provide guidance on ways to enrich and complement your lifestyle through a new lens.'

I grew up straddling several cultures. Born in London to an English father and a Japanese mother, I lived in Seoul, in London and then, for several years, in the cultural melting pot that is New York. But all the while, I always had a strong connection to Japan through my mother and my extended Japanese family, with whom I would spend the sticky, humid summers.

Over the past few years, I've written extensively about Japan on my blog, mostly covering recipes, lifestyle and travel tips. And while I've lived in many places dotted across the globe, I feel as though I always return – in every aspect of my life – to the same frameworks, rituals, habits and traditions: those from my upbringing, family life and time spent in Japan.

The word 'Japonisme' was first used in the late nineteenth century to describe the craze for Japanese art, culture and design in the West – an interest that has grown exponentially in the past few years to include anything from music to film, to food and art.

I think the thing that makes Japan's culture and traditions so uniquely special is its long history of isolation. Japan has acquired such a strong, distinct and rich identity because it lacked external influence for so long. For over 220 years, Japan had an isolationist foreign policy, known as *sakoku*, meaning it was a 'closed country'. Under the Tokugawa shogunate, relations and trade between Japan and the rest of the world were strictly limited. Few were allowed to leave the country, and few were allowed in from the early 1600s, in an attempt to counter the perceived threat of foreign, religious and colonial influence.

Sure, the two-century-long period of national seclusion occurred an *extremely* long time ago, ending in the early 1850s – but that era of solitude, I am convinced, played an enormous part in weaving

INTRODUCTION

the fabric of Japanese society. The customs, tradition and culture of Japan developed and blossomed in that remote bubble and, in my opinion, have made the country we know today quite different from anywhere else in the world. It can be strange, without doubt, and sometimes perplexing too, but it is always intriguing, beautiful and incredibly enlightening. I've been going back there for twenty-six years, and find myself learning something new and different every time, seeing everything afresh, from a novel perspective, over and over again.

So what can be learned from Japanese culture (without getting on a plane)? How can you – like me – apply it to everyday life outside of these tiny little islands? A key lesson for me has been about balance – something I learned from my maternal grandfather, Haruyuki. One of thirteen siblings, from rural farm stock, he rose up the ranks, eventually becoming an influential businessman in his role as Chairman and CEO of Shell in Japan.

His journey began with a chance friendship he struck up with two American soldiers who were stationed in a depressed, post-Second World War Japan. On their recommendation, he set his sights on the United States of America, crossing the Pacific in two weeks on an ocean liner – the *Hikawa Maru* (named after the great Shinto shrine in Saitama). He pursued a bachelor's degree in economics at the University of Washington, supporting himself by working as a gardener, a waiter and a houseboy. As a result of his time in the States, he developed an attitude and approach to business back in Japan that were considered to be fairly unorthodox and distinctly Western. Throughout his life, though, he was fiercely proud of his heritage, and Japanese culture, history and tradition in particular.

It was from my grandfather that I learned the importance of mindfulness – how vital this is for a happy and fulfilling approach and attitude to life. We live in an increasingly connected world, but it comes at a cost. It's hard to switch off when we are constantly bombarded with information and communication, and when it feels like the stress or drama of your working and/or personal life are always looming close at hand (and via push notifications, too).

I learned from my *jiji*'s (grandfather's) example, as he always took the time for self-care; this enabled him to be happy, productive in his working life and to live sustainably. He would spend weekdays in the bustling, vibrant heart of Tokyo with early starts and late nights. But for most of his working life, without fail, he and my grandmother would return at the weekends to Kamakura – a beautiful city by the sea – where he would recharge. He'd spend hours tending the small orange trees in his garden, going on rambling walks in the hills in their neighbourhood, painting, writing poems and painstakingly filleting and preparing fresh fish for dinner. Over the course of my career, during stressful times, I've found myself recharging and getting into the right headspace with similar approaches – creating art (through photography or writing), cooking (filling gyoza dumplings; repetitive, but effective) and organising in different ways (sorting out my wardrobe or putting my papers in order) to help me get into a more grounded and productive mindset.

Later in life, my grandfather grew more and more connected to his spiritual side, becoming actively involved in temple life as an elder. He sat on a council that represented the parishioners at Tsurugaoka Hachimangū, the cultural heart of Kamakura, and its most important Shinto shrine – the place that he loved, cherished and depended on so much when he needed clarity or peace, bringing him back to his tradition and his roots. His work there was important to him. Never one for patronising lectures or filling a silence for the sake of it, every event and ritual he took part in, he filled with appreciation, dedication and meaning.

He was an early riser, getting up to tend to all his plants before being picked up for work. And he'd be my accomplice in sneaking out at 3 a.m. in order to satisfy a jetlag-induced craving for red-bean ice cream at the local *konbini* (convenience store). But always, he would point out the sunrise or the silence of the streets on our walks back home, teaching me how to savour the tiny moments that I would otherwise have missed.

I was in my final year at university in Manchester when my *jiji* died, and it wasn't until I embarked on my own working life that I realised quite how much of his ethos I had taken in and absorbed over the years. Through the tiniest, quietest moments, slightest of actions and the almost imperceptible nuances that he highlighted, I discovered and took in aspects of my own heritage and culture that would shape and guide my life.

Whenever I meet strangers for the first time and tell them about my Japanese heritage and upbringing, the conversation that ensues is always spirited, to say the least, although it does inevitably involve a discussion about their appreciation for anime, for example, or their love of Japanese cuisine and, very occasionally, *karaoke*!

A naturally anxious, cautious person, I've found that there are so many things I draw upon now to help me find clarity, regroup and persevere through challenges, and they are all firmly rooted in Japan and its rich heritage. So it is this that I want to share with you here: not just aspects of Japan and its culture in the abstract, but

Japonisme

Japonisme

philosophies and strategies that have helped me get through some of the hardships, barriers and trials of modern everyday life. In so doing, the process of articulating and distilling the essence of these philosophies and traditions in these pages has renewed my love and appreciation for them, perhaps now more than ever before, making me aware of just how much I really do depend and rely on them in everyday life without even realising it. I hope that they will provide comfort, happiness and food for thought for you too – the kind that can only come from an appreciation of the quieter, yet rich, the ordinary, yet joyful moments along the wider journey.

Part One of the book, '*Kokoro*', focuses on the heart and mind. It is about what drives us to do what we do (*ikigai*) and what brings us joy; the beauty of change (*wabi-sabi*) and of the passing of time; and finding beauty in imperfection and celebrating the hardships and moments that shape us (*kintsugi*). Part Two, '*Karada*', is all about the body: how we engage with our surroundings (through forest bathing, flower arranging and in the home); how we nourish it (through food, tea and bathing); and how we stimulate our minds (through calligraphy). Finally, Part Three, '*Shukanka*' (developing the habit), is about finding ways in which these can all be incorporated into our day-to-day lives and become second nature or routine.

There are so many aspects of Japanese cultural life that I believe can – and should be – adopted more elsewhere. Whether it's changing a mindset, finding time to appreciate a good cup of tea or going out for a brisk walk in nature, these techniques, and others, can really be valuable for all of us who have felt overworked, anxious, haggard, frazzled or rushed. Too often, we get bogged down, stressed and wrung out. We're under constant pressure to

Japonisme

achieve perfection in all that we do, to be happy (never sad, or angry or upset) and to look incredible. We're told that we should do it all and have it all – manage a successful career, while still spending quality time with family, eat well, yet have an amazing body and more. But this approach to life is just too precarious and doesn't take into account the messiness of real everyday life, in which deadlines change, other people can have bad days and take it out on you, or you or your loved ones can become ill. It's extremely high-pressure and stress-inducing. At best, it's unattainable and unrealistic; at worst, it's downright dangerous.

The philosophies I will share with you here and which are so integral to Japanese culture will help you to recognise and deal with the transience of life, to find the beauty within the messy chaos and teach you to adore and cherish your scars – all of which can be so wonderfully freeing. It's about being able to acknowledge that things *will* end, and that things *will* blow up in your face, but without being nihilistic about it. And rather than chasing the unattainable goal of perfection, it's about finding fulfilment and serenity in what already lies in front of you: being able to say, 'I'm not perfect, and it's ok.'

This book is packed with practical tips, suggestions, recipes and more to enhance your current existence – all inspired by the unique, beautiful and magical little islands that are Japan. Just think of the ingredients we used to have to ship over (at great expense), which can now be readily purchased at many local supermarkets; and the intricate bento boxes (painstakingly made for me by my mother), which are now fairly commonplace. These and so many other things are at our disposal now, and by using them, along with making tiny, incremental changes, you will learn how to establish new routines

I   and habits to enrich and complement your lifestyle and wellbeing.
N   This proverb pretty much sums up the thinking that underpins this
T   book. It's through small, iterative steps, rather than the big reveal,
R   that we can make the most significant changes. So take things one
O   step at a time. Many of the arts and practices you will read about,
D   like *ikebana* (see page 116) and tea ceremony (see page 186) take
U   decades to grasp and perfect. Several of my family members have
C   sacrificed countless hours in following and, ultimately, mastering their
T   chosen pursuits, but while I've dipped my toe into many of them, I
I   am by no means an expert. Nor am I a historian or an academic. But
O   through all of them, I have learned something about myself along the
N   way – and that is what I want to share here. Because if I can do it,
then so can you. The hobbies, activities and practices you will read
about will all help to create change; change – and this is key – that is
realistic, practical, affordable and, hopefully, fun, too.

The characters of my last name – Niimi 新美 – mean 'new' and
'beautiful'. My hope is that, through this little book, I will live up to
it, introducing you to new and beautiful Japanese philosophies,
practices and tips to bring just a little bit more mindfulness,
contentment and happiness into your life.

With many
little strokes,
a large tree
is felled.

– *Japanese proverb*

Kokoro

心

The heart and the mind

K
O
K
O
R
O

In Japanese, there are three words to describe the heart. The first is *shinzou*, the physical organ that beats within us all, and keeps us alive. (If a Japanese person tells you that their *shinzou* hurts, they're not speaking metaphorically – get them to a doctor, pronto.) The second is *ha-to*, the shape of a love heart – the kind that you can't escape until late February, once Valentine's Day has passed. The third is *kokoro*.

Heart, mind and soul are inextricably linked in the word *kokoro*. The nearest English equivalent might be conscience; it's a mentality or a feeling and it describes the emotions and desires inside all of us.

Nurturing your *kokoro* is where mindfulness begins, and this applies to every aspect of your life. I've been guilty of prioritising some areas at the expense of others, certainly in my working life. Getting burned out, being terrified of failure, or change, is something that I've struggled with before. But the most important thing I've learned on my journey so far is that failure is inevitable. This realisation has been one of the most liberating of all.

In Part One, I share different outlooks, philosophies and ways of thinking. Whether it's accepting the imperfect, seeing the beauty in things that are broken or finding your motivation, taking the time to care for yourself in more ways than one (paying attention to mental health, as well as physical) will put things in perspective, help you to find joy and enable you to live a fuller, richer, happier life.

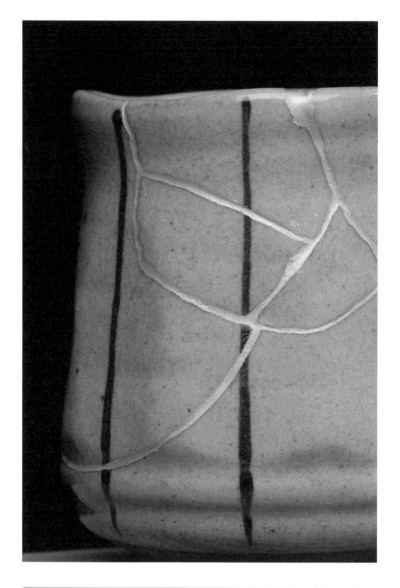

Shortly after my grandfather died, I took my first job out of university in a field I wasn't passionate about. I had moved to London, a city where I didn't know many people, and I lived with a partner who worked so much that they were mostly absent. During this period, I felt lost and adrift.

So I took my camera, and started to document my life in London – the food I ate, what I had enjoyed about my day and things that had made me feel happy at a time when I mostly wasn't. It was starting my blog, following what made me feel good and sharing that part of myself that nourished me and helped me grow.

So first, let's take a look at ways to find your *ikigai*, or purpose – the thing that drives you and makes you get out of bed in the morning. We'll then look at *wabi-sabi* – accepting the nature of impermanence and transience and embracing the presence of chaos in life – before, finally, finding the beauty in the broken, through the art of *kintsugi*.

Ikigai

生き甲斐

Purpose

Ikigai is that thing in our lives that provides a delicious richness – it's what gives life its meaning or, as the French might say, its raison d'être. There is a fire within us all; it may burn brighter in some than in others, and it may waver, but it can also return stronger, hotter and more powerful than ever, and it takes different things to stoke the flames for each of us.

According to a report in 2017 from the World Health Organization, Japan still leads the way for the longest and healthiest life expectancy globally, as it has done for many years.[1] There are, of course, several factors at play. Genetics, diet, lifestyle and an excellent healthcare system can account for most of it. If you ask a Japanese person, though, they would most likely attribute this trend for longevity to a strong work ethic and a certain frame of mind. Many societies can claim to have healthy diets and lifestyles, but the concept of *ikigai*, or purpose, is a key differentiator, and unique to Japanese culture.

After many false starts, my *jiji* (grandfather) finally retired at the age of seventy-three. My whole family, a little naively, assumed this meant we would see more of him during the week. For my *jiji*, though, enjoying his retirement still meant sitting on several boards as a director, giving advice, putting on a suit and having business meetings most days. He loved his work – he used to claim that he did it in order to keep his brain active. For him, his working life was what drove and motivated him – he took a lot of pride in it, and in how he was able to provide for his family as a result. The thought that he might stop working after retirement didn't seem to occur to him. In fact, the only time I ever saw him unsure of himself or wavering in his convictions was whenever he was on the brink of retirement – the concept of idleness, or not working, was something he was extremely suspicious and wary of.

From my own experience, finding your *ikigai* isn't something you come to consciously. It's slowly revealed to you over time, in the moments that help you to get to know yourself. It's never complete, and is constantly in flux. Relatively speaking, I'm still very much in the early stages of my journey, but I do get my *ikigai* through my work. I'm lucky enough to work with incredibly talented and inspirational people, and with causes that are actively helping to make the world a better place. Whether that is through the environment, improving people's lives or making life fairer, the amazing charities that I am involved with make even the day-to-day frustrations worth it (because you can't have the sweet without the bitter).

But the satisfaction and happiness I get from the work that I do wouldn't be possible if I didn't have confidence in myself. I have skills and expertise that I have worked hard to attain, and being able to share them in a small way is what motivates me to keep going, giving my work purpose. I am confident in my ability to do my job, whether that's dealing with clients or through my own blog – and that gives me an immense amount of satisfaction.

But this isn't something that comes easily, and it isn't just about confidence. In fact, it takes a lot of soul-searching, and a lot of failures and a great deal of questioning and self-doubt to get there. Above all, it's about being honest and reflecting on yourself and your behaviour: what makes you happy? What is important to you? Finding the answers to these questions over time can help you to realise what your driver is.

If the current
sinks, it will
rise again.

– *Japanese proverb*

Finding your *ikigai* also calls for balance. As much joy as I get through work, it wouldn't be enough to sustain me. A strong family connection, wonderful friendships and a beautiful little home all contribute towards making my *ikigai* richer and more meaningful. None of this is passively attained though. All relationships require a lot of effort and good communication; sustaining work and home requires compromise; and negativity, self-doubt and hardships are all facts of life. But your *ikigai* is what propels you forward in the darkest moments. Knowing the bad things will pass, and finding that element in your life that helps you achieve contentment is what *ikigai* is all about.

A few years ago, I made it onto a female leadership course where we had to outline our business plan and explain how it would drive our visions. The main thing that resonated with me was that while all our companies might evolve to offer different services over time, the overall vision that took us there, and that we were trying to attain, wouldn't change. That really stuck with me. And the same applies to your *ikigai* as well: just because you know what drives you, doesn't mean you should stay in your comfort zone, and focus on that solely. It's something you can come back to, and you need to be challenged, and push the boundaries. But having a goal and a key driver is important. Think of *ikigai* as the fuel to your motor – you need to make the engine run.

How Do I Find My Ikigai?

Chances are, you already know what makes you happy – you just haven't thought about it as something as grand as your 'purpose for being' (which might sound a little scary). Finding your *ikigai* is at the centre of who you are as a person, and is the result of a combination of factors. We are too often pushed to categorise ourselves into small buckets ('What is your occupation?' or the dreaded dinner-party opener, 'So what is it that you *do*?') or reduce our entire essence or personality down to 140 characters. While it can sometimes be a fun exercise, in reality, we are far too complex for that. There is a saying in Japanese: 'ten people, ten colours'. And the truth is that everyone is different. We all prioritise different things, and one isn't necessarily better than another – so some people may get their *ikigai* through their children, for example, while others get it through their work.

If you think of your life as a flower, then your *ikigai* is the centre, and is what holds it all together. The beauty of the flower comes from the sum of its parts: how beautiful the petals all look together. But individually, each petal represents a different facet in your life, and the things that transcend or tie them all together. One of the petals might be your profession, or your passion – or it could even be what helps you pay the bills each month. How do these facets impact each other? How can they (you) grow and gain strength? What can you improve?

If you try, you may succeed. If you don't try, you will not succeed. This is true of all things. Not succeeding is the result of not trying.

– Japanese proverb

Work

K
I
G
A
I

Admittedly, Japanese working culture doesn't have the best reputation. Office workers in larger corporations are overloaded, the hours are long and there is a distinct lack of work/life balance. These are just some of the criticisms you will often hear, with *karoshi*, or death from overwork, being a real and serious problem in Japanese society that needs addressing.

There are a lot of positives to have come out of the Japanese working culture, though, and I definitely think they are worth bearing in mind and incorporating into your routine.

—Business cards

As someone who works in digital, I will often hand out my business card during a meeting, accompanied by a nervous laugh and a little joke (either, 'Look how Japanese I am!' or a reference to that scene from *American Psycho*, where they all compare their designs).

I ordered my first business card about a month after I graduated from university – all that was on it was my name, email address and mobile phone number.

It may seem like an outdated little ritual, but the number of opportunities that have arisen through handing my business card out has made me a full-blown convert.

Unlike a hastily written thank-you email after a meeting, the kind that will most likely get archived immediately after it's read, a business card acts as a physical reminder of the person whose name is on it. I'm a real fan of the physical and tangible reminder – and a business card is just that.

—Process

We get into the nitty gritty of *kaizen*, or continuous improvement, later on, but suffice to say that many Japanese companies place a lot of focus on the process, and on ongoing improvement. It's why praise doesn't tend to get heaped on employees at Japanese companies – because the job is never really done. There is always something else to be learned; small, continuous improvements that can be made over time.

—Seeing colleagues outside of work

Part of the reason for the work/life balance stigma around Japanese working culture is the focus on *nomikai* – the after-work drinking, karaoke and socialising with colleagues that features so strongly. While I'm a big advocate for work/life balance, I do think there is so much you can get from seeing your co-workers outside work. It helps you build stronger relationships with them, find out a little bit more about what their motivations are and simply see them from another perspective. There's nothing quite like dancing to Madonna with your boss and co-workers at a wedding to bring out a side of them you'd never see at your standard client meeting.

—Otsukaresama – gratitude for work

At the end of a long working day or week, you might say '*otsukaresama*!' to your colleague or friend. *Otsukaresama* directly translates as 'You're tired', but the essence is more about registering another's hard work, and showing your appreciation and gratitude for it: 'You've worked so hard you're tired. I want you to know that it is acknowledged and appreciated.'

Otsukaresama is a tricky one for Westerners because telling someone that they are tired might be misinterpreted. At our weekly Monday-morning meetings, my colleagues and I give each other 'snaps': we highlight small wins and great work from the week before; this usually becomes the best part of our meetings, putting us in the right frame of mind to start the week.

—Self-care

Taking care of yourself is key to productivity. We're not robots. (Well, not quite yet, anyway … That might be something for the next book!)

Taking breaks, in particular, is vital. I find that I am much more productive when I take time out of my schedule to do some exercise – it's so effective at releasing pressure and tension for me, and I always produce better-quality work with a clearer head as a result.

I **Love**

K It makes the world go round, right?

I

G **—Your friendships**

A It's always good to know who will be there to bat for you when times

I are bad. The old adage rings true for me, and that realisation has brought me so much clarity. But remember that friendships need to go both ways, and also to focus on quality, rather than quantity. I've taken more time over the years to focus and cultivate the relationships that are reciprocal, and it's saved me a lot of heartache. Having said that, it's also important to never shut the door on anyone, as you never know what struggles they may be hiding from the outside world.

Friendship is also about being able to have those difficult conversations! Your closest friends are just that because they're not afraid to call you out – and you should, too. If you care about a person, you have a responsibility to hold them accountable (and they you); ultimately, it makes for a stronger bond.

Technology and social media are great tools for maintaining friendships and keeping in contact, but it can feel a little contrived at times. When I was younger, my friends and I would share a *koukan nikki*, or a friendship swap diary, to document our best, worst and funniest moments of the school day. These diaries were readily available, usually with pre-printed categories to be filled in. Each friend would take a day, fill out a page, and pass it on the next day to the next friend. Then, over lunch, when we gathered together, we would share the most hilarious or cringe-inducing of the previous week. While it's not really that sustainable for adult working life, I'm more than a little tempted to bring it back to document our next group holiday (I think it would be perfect at a music festival).

Friends are known first in hardships.

– Japanese proverb

Japonisme

—Your romantic life

There are two ways to define what we mean as 'love' in Japanese: *koi* and *ai*:

• Koi – romantic love

Koi differs from *ai* in that it is mostly driven from the self; it can go in one direction, and can be unreciprocated. Romantic love, longing, desire, wanting, infatuation – these are all '*koi*'.

• Ai – all-encompassing love

Unlike *koi*, which can be selfish, *ai* is not. A parent's love would be described in this way. It is a mutual, unshakeable love. A good way of differentiating the two is that while *koi* is always wanting or seeking, *ai* is always giving.

—The big confession

Unlike most Western relationships (and I'm generalising massively over here), a lot of Japanese romantic relationships start with a big confession, known as *kokuhaku*. Usually, one person will profess their love for the other right at the start, with the intention (and hope) that it is reciprocated. The *kokuhaku* is then either accepted or rejected by the other person. There is something quite refreshing about putting all your cards on the table (even if it does seem like you're coming on a little strong).

Getting a response after a confession of this kind can be a long process, and none more than around the period of 'Valentine's Day' and 'White Day'. On Valentine's Day, people (usually women) give chocolates to the object of their affections. There is then an excruciating month-long wait until White Day (14 March), when they

Japonisme

see what they get in return. The agony of that wait – eek! As if that wasn't already enough of an emotional minefield, you might be the recipient of '*giri-choco*', which refers to chocolate given out of social obligation. Better you than me, my friends.

Family

Family life is incredibly important – and thanks to the long life expectancy in Japan, most families will have very close intergenerational relationships.

—Remembering those that have gone

The way family members and ancestors are memorialised in Japan keeps the presence and impact they had in life alive, and also helps to give them a role, even after their passing. Most homes will have a *butsudan*, or a small shrine, dedicated to a lost loved one, with candlesticks, a bell, incense and a platform on which to place offerings in the form of food, like rice or tea.

Immediately after a relative has died, there are several ceremonies that take place, as well as annually, on the anniversary of their death, until the fiftieth year. While it might sound a tad morbid, in reality it is an incredibly lovely way of remembering someone. Once the formal ceremony has taken place, recounting memories of that person and their impact on your life is a beautiful and wonderful thing. Rather than tears of grief, I usually end up doubled over in fits of laughter over hilarious memories (which is the reaction I'm sure I'd want to leave behind). This tradition is one I've carried over to my English family, too, usually over a Sunday roast dinner around the time of my late British grandfather's birthday.

Environment

Finding contentment and happiness in your surroundings is a massive contributor to your overall happiness. We are, after all, the products of our environment.

—Cleaning up

It still amazes me every time I go back to Japan how little litter there is in the centre of Tokyo, especially given that there never seems to be a rubbish bin around when I need one! Respect for communal space is strongly ingrained in the Japanese, and cigarette smokers will even walk around with portable ashtrays, so they don't litter the streets.

—Home

There are entire YouTube channels dedicated to the way clothes are folded in Japan, and a focus on de-cluttering and organisation are definitely an important part of daily life. They save time, make you more efficient and look better – in my opinion, *everyone* needs to get on board with this one.

Respect

It's when I take public transport in Japan that I notice the level of respect for others the most. The majority of people will switch their phones to 'manner mode' (a silent, non-disruptive setting), conversations take place in subdued tones and people are always quick to give up their seat to anyone whose need is greater. Could someone please send this memo to Transport for London?

While I'm on the subject, if you see someone who needs a seat, be sure to stand up for them. And even if you can't offer them a seat, you can always ask loudly if they need one (that way, other passengers usually look up from their phones).

—Respecting your elders

Elderly relatives tend to move in with their younger ones, and having several generations living under one roof is a fairly common phenomenon. There is a lot of cultural cache in respecting your elders – so much so that there's even a day dedicated to it (the third Monday of September every year, known as Respect for the Aged Day).

Self

In order to keep motivated, and work most effectively, self-care and achieving balance are so important. In the past, I've been guilty of neglecting this and the fallout has been less than pretty. Keeping active, eating well, keeping your mind fit and reflecting on your actions are all vital parts of self-care, and are just as important as the other stuff.

—Cycling

Cycling in Japan is an absolute joy. I found cycling in Kyoto in particular so much fun, and the best way to explore the sprawling city from temple to temple. You tend to find everyone – from kids to little old ladies – on their bikes, and usually without the need for helmets or lights, as drivers tend to give cyclists the room and respect they need to cycle safely. And it's not uncommon to see bikes parked outside train stations unlocked, as their owners commute to work confident in the belief that their bike will most likely be there when they return. While I wouldn't recommend going without helmets or lights, or leaving your bike unchained, cycling is a great way to keep fit and active and to get from A to B, while saving money and doing your bit for the environment.

Work
of self,
obtainment
of self.

— *Japanese proverb*

—Calisthenics

Calisthenics, or *radio taiso*, are broadcast on NHK (the national broadcaster) public radio around 6.30 a.m. every single day. The movements are gentle, and seem to become ingrained in your psyche (even mine, and I have two left feet, no sense of rhythm and terrible muscle memory for movement).

It's pretty common for *radio taiso* to be used at school as part of a warm-up for gym or PE class, but many companies still get their employees to practise it, too. Getting your muscles going in the morning can really help you wake up and stay focused. You can even do most of the moves sitting down, so there really is no excuse not to do it!

—Sudoku

An important part of self-care is keeping your brain engaged and on top fighting form. *Sudoku* is one of the ways in which you can do this.

Sudoku is a logic-based puzzle, in which you have to place numbers between one and nine in every line and box within nine three-by-three grids, without repeating any numbers within the grids or the columns.

—Haiku

If numbers aren't your thing, then maybe words are. Challenge and stimulate yourself intellectually by writing *haiku*: follow a three-line format, in which the first and last lines have five syllables and the middle has seven. Within these constraints, try and juxtapose two ideas or sensory images. These could be colours, sounds, flavours, or temperatures, possibly set against emotions like love, fear, anger or joy. The juxtaposition should help to create the mood, or atmosphere, between the 'human' and 'natural' worlds, for example, or to reference a time of year or season without explicitly saying when it is.

A *haiku* typically should elicit an emotional response, or evoke a feeling of some kind. It's a subtle art, and emotions should be conveyed subtly, rather than being stated bluntly or overtly. Like putting together a menu, referencing the time of year, or seasons, usually goes down well. Write from personal experience – it should be sincere; so if you've never worked a day in the mines, then a *haiku* about a hard day down the mines kind of defeats the purpose.

In a way, I feel like all writing is created to be read (otherwise, what are we doing it for?), but in many ways a *haiku* can feel too personal – and working within the constraints of brevity, subtlety and seasonality are challenging enough without having the added pressure to share. Don't feel you have to do so, if you don't want to – there is something luxurious and a little indulgent about creating it for your eyes only.

—Gratitude

Having a positive attitude and demeanour can make such a difference in all of your relationships, professional or otherwise. It's easier said than done, though, and on those days when nothing seems to be going your way, you can all too readily let those minor annoyances build up and get to you.

I've been keeping a gratitude journal for a while now, and it really does work wonders. I write three things a day I've felt grateful for, including the days when it's seemed hopeless, I've always found something, even if it is as mundane as hanging my clothes outside to dry. Here are some sample entries from some of the bad days:

- Grateful for pineapple
- Grateful for going to the gym
- Grateful for early nights

They are so much fun to read (and now I can't even remember what was so horrible about that day in the first place).

One who smiles
rather than
rages is always
the stronger.

– Japanese proverb

The prime of
your life does not
come twice.

– Japanese proverb

—Up and at 'em!

The word '*ganbare*' encapsulates the spirit of how to summon up motivation. It's a combination of 'do your best' and 'don't give up', and captures the enthusiasm and passion you need to keep going sometimes – to keep the end goal in sight.

Ganbare represents an attitude, or the spirit of determination and perseverance. You might hear it chanted at marathons, for example, as an expression of encouragement and solidarity.

Finding your purpose and your *ikigai* can help you find contentment in that it allows you to be more focused. Rather than being distracted or consumed by the smaller daily frustrations we all encounter, your *ikigai* brings the most important aspects to the fore and, in so doing, it can help you let go. It can also help you to be more empathetic towards others, realising that everyone is motivated differently, and that one way isn't necessarily more 'right' or more valid than another.

Ultimately, finding your *ikigai* can help you to be more productive with your time, by paying attention to the most important aspects of your life – whether that's building a home, spending time with your family or getting to where you want to be in your career.

Wabi-sabi

侘寂

The beauty of imperfection and impermanence

More than anything else in this book, *wabi-sabi* as a worldview, an aesthetic and a way of life has been the hardest to pin down and translate.

The original meaning of *wabi* referred to the feeling of remote loneliness that comes with living in nature, and the paradoxical beauty of imperfection (like a broken cup fixed with gold, through *kintsugi*).

Sabi, depending on the context, can mean 'withered', 'lean' or 'cooled', but more often refers to the beauty of ageing – like the changing hue of wood, the comeliness of rust, the delicate droop and drying of roses in the sun.

In many ways, it's simpler to convey the essence of what *wabi-sabi* is in contrast to what it *isn't*:

- Asymmetry, not conformity or evenness
- Humble and modest, not arrogant, conceited or proud
- Growth, not stagnation
- Natural decay, not synthetic or preserved
- Slow, not fast
- Abstemious, not gluttonous
- Not hampered by materials, not materialistic
- Dignified, not indecorous
- Minimal, not ostentatious
- Rustic, not polished
- Withered, not fresh
- Fluid, not inflexible
- Unfinished, not complete
- Small moments, not grand gestures

Wabi-sabi, to me, is being inside when it's raining outside; the laughter lines on a face; or feeling pleasantly sated after a simple lunch.

In Beauty

The *wabi-sabi* aesthetic and approach to beauty means accepting the natural ageing process – wrinkles will come, creases will appear – and being able to recognise, remember and find happiness in the moments that have passed.

There is a dental-surgery trend to which many Japanese women subscribe in order to attain their version of a 'perfect smile'. It is called *yaeba*, and paradoxical though it may be, it is actually a smile that is crooked, out of line. The beauty in *yaeba* is that it represents the vivacity of youth, and the idea that an imperfect, snaggle-toothed smile is endearing and beautiful as a result of its flaws.

In the Home

In terms of bringing the *wabi-sabi* aesthetic into the home, it's worth thinking about it in this way: it's about the threadbare couch, not the white leather sofa; the mucky fingerprints on the wall; the port wine stain on the new carpet. Home is a lived-in space, not a showroom. Minimalist, free of clutter, and natural; it has a place in our world, makes reference to nature, but is not sterile, bland and without character or humour.

Many Japanese homeware stores sell items that are rustic and simply decorated – where the wood is unpainted, and is the central feature. Like a fine wine, wood gets better and more interesting over time, as it begins to tell stories and takes on a character of its own.

WABI-SABI

In Objects

I always find using brand new objects, particularly things like new leather bags, somewhat unsettling and uncomfortable. I have to get used to things, and they have to get used to me – they need to become part of my narrative, in the same way that I need to become part of their life cycle.

At a music festival several years ago, a bottle of hand sanitiser leaked all over a new designer wallet I had saved up and purchased for myself as a birthday gift. I was disappointed, frustrated and angry at the time, but it has ended up as a reminder of dancing by my tent in the sweltering heat, staying up until 5 a.m. listening to incredible artists and making questionable decisions fuelled by misjudged shots of rakija – all stories woven into the fabric of my life and physically manifested in a dark stain on a battered old purse.

In Time

Whenever anyone asks me the best time of year to go to Japan, I never know how to answer – because every season has its unique advantages. The cherry blossoms are out in the spring, but the summer offers shaved ices, Bon Festival and fireworks. The autumn boasts incredible foliage while the delights of Japanese winters include warm *sake*, snow and, if you're lucky, red-crowned cranes.

The passage of time, of growth, decay and death, and appreciating the natural order of events, is also a key part of *wabi-sabi*. Finding contentment, mindfulness and appreciation for all of this is at the heart of what *wabi-sabi* is as a concept and mindset; it is a way of life and of understanding the world around us.

In What We Already Have

Wabi-sabi is not about having the latest thing or acquiring new objects; it's about rediscovering an old top at the back of your wardrobe or making a tasty meal with the detritus in your fridge. In fact, it's not about material possessions, or owning anything at all. Frugal doesn't seem like the most appropriate word to use here, and nor does thrifty – because it's more about being canny and prudent and making do. And it's about finding satisfaction, contentment and happiness by doing so.

Part of this has to do with the mentality that comes with living in a place so fraught with earthquakes, tsunamis and other natural disasters. Quite simply, you learn to let go.

In Ageing

Perhaps because of the large (and growing ever larger) elderly population, the concept of ageing in Japan isn't something that is shied away from quite so much as it is, perhaps, in the West. Life in Japan seems to be a bit more inclusive for the older generation. This even happens in a digital context, where the group and demographic are better catered for. There is an extensive and constantly evolving selection of smartphones designed specifically with the older user in mind, for example.

The older generation hold a position of respect within the community, and caring for them is viewed as a communal, societal responsibility. Perhaps this is why the concept of ageing well and gracefully is so clearly apparent in Japan – because of the way caring for the elderly is approached culturally.

Japonisme

This relates closely to the concept of *fureai* – the mutual connection or bond that is formed between generations, or across different professions or vocations within society. *Fureai*, which means 'a close mutuality', is different from a more traditional relationship or friendship. It is used to describe the relationship a kindergarten teacher might have with their charges or a nurse might have with the patients under their care.

It is within this kind of environment that things like *fureai kippu* (a 'caring relationship ticket') can take hold and flourish. Introduced in the early 1990s, a *fureai kippu* became a form of social currency or credits representing an hour of community service that can be earned, credited or exchanged. This could be peer-to-peer, within the same generational group (where friends might help each other out with tasks like popping to the pharmacy, for example), or between generations in return for errands, like being driven somewhere, or assisted with certain chores. So a younger person might earn these credits by driving someone to the shop, helping with weeding the garden or physical or manual labour that an elderly person is unable to do themselves.

People with elderly family elsewhere are able to assist in their own local community and then transfer their credits to their relatives so that they, in turn, can access similar services that traditionally might have been provided by their family, had they lived closer.

Fureai kippu is, ultimately, a physical, tradeable manifestation of altruism, in a bankable, swappable form. Some beneficiaries of the *fureai kippu* system prefer services obtained through the community, rather than those driven by purely financial means, due to the perceived (if not slightly contrived) personal connection.

The bottom line is that ageing isn't something to be scared of or to shy away from – it happens to all of us. The lessons here that can be learned are about respect, compassion and helping to build a stronger, more thoughtful and welcoming community for everyone, at every stage of their journey.

In Living Life Unfiltered

As someone who earns their keep by advising charities about the incredible and amazing things they can do with social media, I know first-hand about how damaging it can be as well.

There is a constant pressure to post about how happy your life is, how much fun you're having or how great you're looking – all the while being surrounded by others doing the same. But it's important to remember to take it all with a pinch of salt. No one likes talking about their bad days or their aches and scrapes; be conscious that everything isn't always as rosy beneath the surface as it appears to be elsewhere – and always be kind.

All of this ties into a larger pattern about the transience of life, the fickleness of being human and how quickly life passes you by. Try to always be present, be real, be yourself. You'll be happier that way.

Shibui

Many objects that are *wabi* or *sabi* can also be considered to be *shibui*. This can be translated as a muted, understated and sophisticated, yet modest or subdued kind of beauty that hints at a deeper complexity within, despite being seemingly simple upon first glance.

The word behind the concept translates to being astringent or sharp, but not necessarily with a negative connotation. Many things can be *shibui*, in that they are direct, unassuming, uncomplicated. And it is in their very functionality that the beauty and appeal lie.

Austerity is another word that could be used to convey the feeling behind *shibui*, but it includes an element of elegance and grace as well. *Shibui* colours, for example, are subdued – greyer tones, in particular.

It's about enjoying the simpler things in life – without being overindulgent, or overly extravagant, and finding the beauty and charm in the distressed, well-worn item of clothing, and how it can bring joy.

Mono No Aware – the Bittersweet Nature of Being

'*Mono*' means thing, and '*aware*' (pronounced ah-wah-re) translates to the sensitivity or gentle sadness about the transitory, ephemeral nature of life. It can also mean sensitivity towards things and the nature of life – something that is consciously recognised and accepted with a hint of melancholy or wistfulness.

This is another way in which the Japanese language manages to capture a feeling that we have all had. I recently had a conversation with a friend at a dinner party, who pointed out that at one point in your childhood, your parent would have picked you up or lifted you onto their shoulders for the last time – and *mono no aware* perfectly encapsulates the feeling that thought evokes. It's a sadness at that realisation, but also an acknowledgment of the inevitability of it all. It comes from reflection and self-awareness and from observing the wider world around you.

Natsukashii

For the first few days of a visit back to Japan I can always be heard to make frequent exclamations of '*natsukashii*'!

Natsukashii is a feeling of nostalgic happiness, or something that evokes an emotion or a memory of some kind. It mostly happens when I come across a specific scent or eat something familiar that I haven't had in a while.

The sentiment behind *natsukashisii*, while mostly one of happiness, is ever so slightly tinged with a wistful poignancy, too. On balance, however, it's a happy and enjoyable feeling, and the kind you want to experience when you are down. You might get it when seeing old school friends or thinking of old habits or activities you might have phased out of your life. Flicking through old albums or listening to songs from a certain time in your life, for example, is a great way to bring comfort and take stock.

I think *wabi-sabi* appeals to so many outside of Japan as a concept because it contrasts with other ideals of perfection – relentlessly pursuing youth, being static or being without flaws. In many ways, those ideals are completely unrealistic and unattainable, and almost without grace. Finding comfort and beauty in the passing of the moment, and being relaxed in accepting that which we cannot change, seems more forgiving. It makes finding peace and contentment attainable and encourages you to be more observant and kinder to yourself.

Wabi-sabi brings you back to the essence of what it means to be human, and your relationship with natural processes and the journey that you are on – how quickly life sneaks up on you and how important it is to count your blessings.

Kintsugi

金継ぎ

Finding beauty in imperfection

According to legend, the art of *kintsugi* (or *kintsuguroi*), meaning 'connecting with gold', can be attributed to the fifteenth-century shogun Ashitaga Yoshimasa, who was so dismayed at a botched repair job to one of his prized ceramic pieces that he implored some Japanese craftsmen to come up with another, more aesthetically pleasing, solution. The art of *kintsugi* was developed as a response to this.

The Philosophy behind Kintsugi

Kintsugi is the art of repairing broken pottery with golden lacquer. Shattered pieces are put back together, and become even more beautiful laced with gold than they were originally. Rather than being discarded or lamented for its flaws, an object becomes more treasured than ever, as its disfigurement or defect becomes its strength through the art of *kintsugi*, adding to its beauty.

Kintsugi can often be found in the cups used for tea ceremony (or *sado*), where pieces with an interesting imperfection or defect are prized for their beauty and aesthetic quality.

The concept of *kintsugi* is a compelling metaphor and doesn't only have to apply to objects. It's an important and even empowering one to think about, particularly at those times in your life that are challenging. It can even apply to something as trivial as a characteristic or 'flaw' you perceive in yourself. For example, I've always had a freckly face. I have spent countless hours and hundreds of pounds on products to cover and conceal the blemishes that seem to appear across my face whenever I've been out in the sun for too long.

Growing up, there was always one freckle in particular that I hated – on my chin, slightly off centre, just to the left. I'd cover it completely with product in an attempt to make it vanish, which it never quite did, much to my dismay.

Then, during my first year of university – an incredibly awkward time of life when you're trying to make friends and find your feet in a new city and surroundings – someone who would later become one of my closest friends, mentioned how much she liked this hated freckle. It was just a passing remark, made as we were getting ready for a night out, but ever since, that mark on my chin has always made me think of her, of that time in my life and of how much fun we have together. It transformed that freckle from a blemish to one of my favourite features.

I love the philosophy behind *kintsugi* because the hardships we face really do shape who we are as people. In the same way that you need the bitter in order to taste the sweet, the struggles we all face – loss, betrayal, heartbreak, disappointment – are a part of our histories, our identities and our stories. And rather than hiding the scars that they leave, *kintsugi* encourages us to celebrate them, and the ways in which they serve to define us. Nothing is ever truly broken, no matter how painful it might seem at the time.

On a more practical level, it also encourages us to be more mindful and conscious consumers. Instead of indulging in fast fashion, we should take care of our possessions, focusing on the process of repair, rather than instinctively discarding and replacing with something new. It's better for the environment, better for our bank accounts and it cuts down on clutter too.

Conversely, *kintsugi* also serves as a powerful metaphor for the way we approach our perceived strengths and weaknesses. There is a Japanese proverb that captures this so perfectly – *chousho wa tansho*, which loosely translates to 'Our strengths are our weaknesses'. Overreliance on or overconfidence about our perceived strengths can catch us when we least expect it.

It's an important lesson to not take the things we consider as strengths for granted – they all require work, dedication and a great deal of cultivation, whether it's a skill, a relationship or our health (mental and physical).

It is finding joy and beauty in imperfection, and celebrating it, that makes *kintsugi* so powerful.

Japonisme

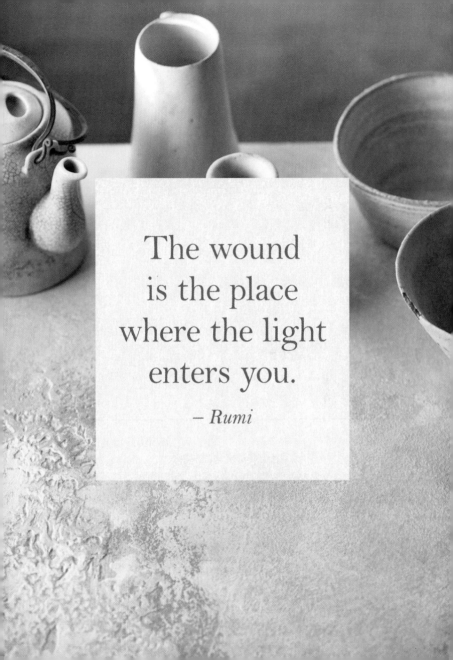

The wound
is the place
where the light
enters you.

– *Rumi*

Types of Kintsugi

There are several ways to repair broken ceramics using the *kintsugi* method.

—Fixing the crack: hibi

This is for smaller breaks or hairline fractures, as it requires the least amount of effort and use of gold resin. It's perfect for those breaks where you still have all of the pieces, and they can be easily put back together. No overlap is required; it's just a question of placing the broken pieces together and sealing with the gold-dusted lacquer.

—Replacing with gold: kake no kintsugi rei

For breaks where pieces are missing, or don't fit back together quite so well, you would seal the broken areas with a larger piece of gold.

—Patchwork: yobi tsugi

Here, missing pieces are replaced with pieces from another, different, broken object, like a patchwork.

Mending Pottery the Kintsugi Way

Traditional, authentic *kintsugi* is done using real gold – and it takes practice, precision and a whole host of skills. However, if you're keen to take a stab at it, you can also buy *kintsugi* kits quite easily online to do at home (although the gold might not be real). They usually include:

- Glue or resin
- Putty
- Gold powder
- A thin paintbrush

You would mix the glue or resin with the gold powder and paint it onto one side of the broken object. Then, working quickly, press the connecting piece into place, using the resin to bind the object together. While you should act swiftly when painting and holding, when it comes to releasing or letting go, take your time and ensure that the pieces have connected properly.

If you are repairing a bigger piece, like *kake no kintsugi rei*, mix some of the gold powder with the putty to seal the missing area.

Applying the Kintsugi Philosophy to Your Life

We know that *kintsugi* goes beyond mending the physical breaks in pottery or ceramics, but just how can we make it a part of our day-to-day lives? Here are a few ways in which to incorporate it:

—Don't rest on your laurels

It's natural for us to focus on our weaknesses, and try to improve them, but don't take your strengths for granted or neglect them. You might be caught out if you do.

—Repair, don't replace

Just because an object is broken, doesn't mean it's come to the end of its useful life. Shoes are a great example – take them to a cobbler to mend the heels. (And invest in quality at the outset, rather than buying a cheap pair that will inevitably fall apart.)

—Embrace your flaws and imperfections

They are what make us different and define us. Also, rather than striving to meet unrealistic standards (which will leave you constantly disappointed), focus on what you like about yourself. Framing things in a positive way can improve your outlook and, ultimately, give you more contentment.

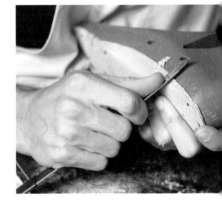

A Metaphor for Life

Kintsugi is so beautiful because it really highlights a pivotal moment in the life of an object – the point at which it may crack under pressure. But it also shows that the object can still retain its magnificence – that the moment at which it cracks is merely a small step in a longer, more important journey.

Kintsugi can be considered as a metaphor for overcoming loss or betrayal, bringing to light not the loss itself, but how it shaped the object or person in question. It plays an important role in tea ceremony, and reveals so much about the psyche and cultural values within that process – tea cups with *kintsugi*, and other

so-called flaws and imperfections, are prized over those that are supposedly flawless. The flaws, chips, repairs and cracks reveal a lot more about the owner's relationship with the objects as well: how well taken care of they are, how loved, how they are depended upon and the integral part they play within someone's practice.

Part of all this is in the eye of the beholder, but it can also be analogous to the relationship someone might have with their childhood teddy. It will never be as beautiful to another person, who doesn't have that intense relationship with it – yet it will be obvious to see, from the patchwork, the repairs, and worn materials, that the object is loved, and that it has played a significant role in the life of its owner.

Shoganai

The attitudes and ideology behind the concept of *kintsugi* are brought about by a willingness and increased flexibility to accept the things that cannot be changed. The word for this is *shoganai*, which means 'it cannot be helped'. Didn't manage to get the last loaf from the bakery? *Shoganai.* Didn't get the role you wanted in the play you auditioned for? *Shoganai.* It's about acknowledging your disappointment, but also knowing that nothing else can be done. It sucks, and let's just recognise that, before moving on.

> As Part One comes to a close, remember that nurturing your *kokoro*, or heart, mind and soul, isn't something that someone else can do for you. Others can play an important role, helping you along the way, but, ultimately, the responsibility lies with you. You need to carve out the time to take care of yourself in order to help others, and to be more productive. Again, it's all about balance, but be sure to make time for it.
>
> Find your driver and your purpose, your *ikigai*. Aim high, but be realistic; know your limits, but then test them. Remember to take your time, and celebrate the little milestones – time is fleeting, and will rush past you sooner than you know. Stay humble, be fluid and take the time to reflect.
>
> You will face hardships – you'll almost certainly get bumps and scratches along the way. But those are the things that will shape you – and celebrating those scars will show you just how far you have come.

02

Karada

体

The body

K
A
R
A
D
A

Contentment and mindfulness are often achieved through ritual and practice. By going through the motions and by letting your creative juices flow, you can find clarity – bringing things into perspective and focus.

Whether it's going for a walk, making tea, arranging flowers – these simple actions and many more can reveal so much about who you are and about your relationships, not only with others, but with yourself.

I called this section *karada*, or the body, because it's all about the physical – through movement, through art or by taking in your immediate environment and surroundings.

I never thought of myself or my family as being particularly traditional, but I was pleasantly surprised when I began to write this section to realise just how much Japanese traditions and customs have, in fact, been incorporated into our daily lives: my grandfather's wanderings around his much-loved Kamakura Highland area, among the mountains and hills; my Aunt Junko's forays into the art of flower arranging (*ikebana*); my grandmother, Motoko's, love of calligraphy; and my mother's younger sister, Taeko's, lifelong practice of tea ceremony.

Food is a big passion of mine. It's what made me begin writing about and sharing my experiences in the first place, and it's something I got from my mother, a keen and skilled cook. Speaking to my family about why they loved calligraphy, *ikebana* and tea ceremony, and valued *shinrin-yoku* (forest bathing), and how it all fits into their busy and chaotic lives, made me appreciate it all so much more than I ever did before.

Done in the traditional and authentic way, these Japanese arts and practices require years of dedication, learning from masters in their respective fields and a great deal of investment, of both money

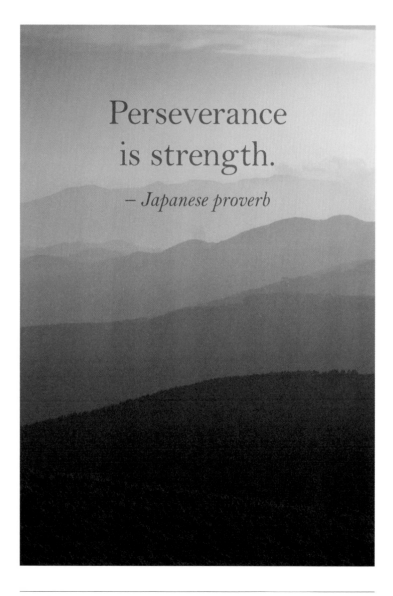

Perseverance
is strength.

– Japanese proverb

Japonisme

and time. Like all good things, they can't be rushed, but it's definitely worth persevering. Becoming an advanced practitioner in an ancient Japanese art like *ikebana* or tea ceremony is probably out of reach for most of us on a practical level (unless you are based in Japan), but there are so many things we can learn, adapt and incorporate into our lives on a smaller, more realistic (not to mention more convenient) level.

In Part Two, we'll take a look at the benefits behind well-known activities like *shinrin-yoku*, *ikebana* and *onsen*, bathing in hot springs, as well as things like our approach to food, and what you can learn about the way it is done in Japan. The aim is, through all these and other practices, like calligraphy, to find inspiration for how you can shape your surroundings, transform your home and learn to appreciate the smaller things (such as how satisfying a good cup of tea can be).

Taking the time to get to know yourself is vital, and these arts and practices are just some of the ways in which you can do so. Many of them, like flower arranging, forest bathing or calligraphy, are more solitary pursuits. They put you in touch with yourself, but can also be shared with others (they can be put on display, discussed or brought into a wider community or network). If you aren't able to take the time for yourself, you won't be able to help others effectively; it's about knowing and believing that it is not selfish or indulgent to prioritise this aspect of your life.

Shinrin-yoku

森林浴

Nourished by nature

S
H
I
N
R
I
N
-
Y
O
K
U

Shinrin-yoku is a term originally coined by the Japanese Ministry for Agriculture in the 1980s to describe the practice of healing through being immersed in nature, or 'forest bathing'.

Countless scientific studies have proven the importance of being surrounded by nature and trees, and the practice is widely accepted as having tangible therapeutic value. It doesn't take a scientist to tell you that going on a walk can help improve your overall health, but it's the mindset you go in with that makes the practice of *shinrin-yoku* so effective.

Although I now live in central London, I walk *everywhere*. Whether it's by the canals or crossing the bustling pavements of the bridge over the Thames to get to work, it helps me get into the right headspace and is often the highlight of my mornings. Feeling the sun on your face or the wind in your hair, even if only for a little bit, can be so refreshing. This is the feeling that you are chasing through *shinrin-yoku*: being healed by nature. And it works wonders.

There is a phrase in Japan – another one of those seemingly untranslatable aphorisms: *kachou fuugetsu*. Separately, the characters are 'flower, bird, wind and moon', but together, they are greater than the sum of their parts, describing something far more powerful and emotive. *Kachou fuugetsu* most commonly translates as learning about yourself through experiencing the beauty of nature. I think there is something so charming – almost restorative – in that sentiment: knowing your place in the world and taking it back to basics.

Ideally, you want to be surrounded by greenery – trees, in particular. Japan is home to some beautiful forests, and the Japanese are famous for their gardens. Think of being out in nature as being similar to your daily allocation of fruit or vegetables; it's a type of nourishment or medicine, counteracting your hectic and stressful day-to-day or nine to five.

Your Six-step Guide to Shinrin-yoku

1. Leave your devices at home

In order to be properly immersed in nature, and get the full benefits of *shinrin-yoku*, you need to switch off (and that means from Instagram, too) all devices from mobile phones to fitness trackers – anything that is going to send you push notifications or detract from being in the moment, causing your mind to wander elsewhere. Stay in the forest, both physically and mentally. Whatever it is that is beckoning you from elsewhere, it can wait until your return.

2. Don't follow a set path

Taking in your surroundings – the sights, sounds and smells – is all part of the healing process. You don't want to be distracted or become stressed, flustered or obsessed with following a set path or seeing a particular landmark or site. Leave the ordnance survey maps at home. If you do stumble across that landmark on your way, that's great – but it's not an essential part of the excursion.

3. Soak up the atmosphere

Actively engage with the landscape around you, and keep your eyes off your watch. Identify different plant or tree varieties, count the number of rings in the trunk of a tree . . . *Shinrin-yoku* isn't about getting from A to B, but savouring the moments and the stillness along the way. It's about wandering without a fixed destination. But don't confuse not having a fixed destination with not having a purpose because there is one. It's just about getting you somewhere in your mind, rather than your body.

4. Quiet, please!

If you go with others, make a pact to spend some time in silence, to allow for quiet reflection and to centre yourself. Listen to your mind and your body, and connect with nature contemplatively; don't use it as an opportunity for a proper catch up. (That can come later, perhaps, over a cup of tea.)

5. Practise mindfulness

Try to leave your emotional baggage at home. Or, if you are unable to, address each issue one at a time. The aim here is to achieve clarity, and to use this time as an escape. After a mental break, you will be able to see things more clearly.

6. Take five, or ten, or twenty . . .

It's not a hike, or a test of your endurance. Take frequent breaks, and soak it all in. Didn't I tell you to leave that fitness tracker at home?

Natural Phenomena You Might Notice on Your Path

Not being able to see the forest for the trees is an expression I'm sure we've all used time and time again, but through *shinrin-yoku* you want to do just that. Take in the details you haven't noticed before, and take the time to observe and seek out the details, looking at everything in a new light. There are so many Japanese words that explain the relationships between different phenomena in a single word, and I think they are too beautiful not to share – something to look out for next time you're off to bathe in the forest.

—Komorebi

There are some beautiful words in the Japanese language that don't have a direct English translation, as we've seen, and *komorebi* might be one of my favourites. It's used to describe the kind of light you see in a forest – the rays of sun that are filtered through the leaves of the trees.

—Kogarashi

Another word that I think conveys so much about the subtleties of nature and how they are observed is *kogarashi* – used to describe a cold, wintry wind. This doesn't refer to a bitter gale, however. It's the kind of wind that nudges the leaves off the trees. *Kogarashi* denotes the leaf wilting process, and focuses on a specific time of year and, more specifically, the phenomenon of leaves falling off the trees.

—Kawaakari

This is the word for the way light – particularly moonlight – reflects off a river, expressing the shimmers, ripples and gleams. It refers to the brightening of the river, and the way the light plays with the surface.

The Science behind Shinrin-yoku

Shinrin-yoku is not just hippie, new-age nonsense. The benefits are backed up by science (hooray for book facts). In addition to a good walk being good for your cardiovascular health, studies have looked into some of the other advantages. *Shinrin-yoku* has been shown to lower the concentration of cortisol (the stress hormone), as well as pulse rate and blood pressure.[2]

Part of this can be attributed to the fact that trees release compounds called phytoncides, which you'd inhale during a walk in the woods. A study in 2009 found that these phytoncides helped to increase and stimulate the activity of white blood cells called 'natural killer cells'. These cells help to fight infection, and are critical for a healthy immune system.[3] The smell of cedar can, apparently, provide some positive effects, too.

Japonisme

Shinrin-yoku in the City

If you are lucky enough to live in a city with green spaces, take advantage of them. Try and get out of the office on your lunch breaks, and go for a brief walk outside. Even if it's only for ten minutes, it will do you a world of good. And while you're out there, why not volunteer? Plant some bulbs, do a little weeding or trim some hedges – you can reap the benefits of *shinrin-yoku* while helping your local community, too.

Although *shinrin-yoku* is all about being in nature, around greenery, not all of us are able to get out into nature so easily. But there are other ways to incorporate it into your life – perhaps by planning to get out of the city several times a year, or even into manmade green spaces, like greenhouses or botanical gardens, if only for an hour or two.

Bringing Nature Indoors

There is a whole chapter dedicated to the art of *ikebana* flower arrangement (see page 116), but you can definitely bring nature indoors in other ways, too. I grew up in a house full of plants, and I usually end up spending a small fortune at a flower market I'm lucky enough to live within walking distance of (and where you can find me most Sundays).

—Miniature bonsai trees

Bonsai are perhaps the best-known Japanese houseplants, but they do require a bit of tender, loving care. Water them when the soil is slightly dry, and cover the roots – but not too much, as you don't want to soak the plant. Making sure you have the right soil mixture is also key, as the goal is to retain moisture. Damp soil is what you are aiming for. Prune the plant regularly, once the shoots have grown a couple of centimetres.

—Bamboo shoots

Water sparingly. Don't drown them.

The type of container you keep your bamboo in also has an impact. Thinking about keeping it in water? Add a few pebbles, and keep it in a clear container. Use a ceramic one if you're thinking of potting it in soil, but make sure there is drainage. Think about the aesthetic you prefer, but also be realistic about maintenance – a clear container is more likely to grow algae.

Keep your bamboo out of direct sunlight, but in a light and bright room. Keep it neat: trim and remove yellowing leaves. And when picking a plant, go for green.

—Regal chrysanthemums

Although Japan is most famous for its cherry blossoms, the chrysanthemum, or *kiku*, is the flower that features in the imperial seal of Japan. Representing rejuvenation and longevity, the flower is emblazoned across every Japanese passport as the symbol of the nation.

Chrysanthemums tend to really flourish outdoors; indoors, they are less likely to bloom for very long, but they do make great gifts. Don't forget to 'deadhead' the plants, and also take off any dead leaves and flowers you might come across. This will extend their shelf life, and look nicer too.

—Azaleas

Keep it cool! This will make the azaleas last longer in an indoor environment. Don't be tempted to re-pot your azalea plants, as the restricted roots are a good thing. And avoid keeping them in draughty rooms.

Creating a Japanese-inspired Garden

Japanese gardens have inspired and captured the imagination of Western art and culture; almost every major Western European capital will be home to a Japanese garden of some kind.

Once built, a Japanese garden can be fairly low maintenance, particularly when a rock garden constitutes a key feature. To lend a little Japanese-inspired flair to your garden, consider including the following:

- **A winding path.** Winding stone paths are common in Japanese gardens, symbolically representing the journey through life.

- **Lanterns.** Japanese *tōrō* (or 'light basket') lanterns were traditionally only used in Buddhist temples as offerings to Buddha. They come in several varieties – they can be hanging or little pagoda-style ones on the ground. Stone, bronze or wooden ones can be found in many gardens today, the most common being the stone lanterns that illuminate paths on the ground.

- **Rock gardens.** Easy to maintain, a rock garden with larger stones throughout can look incredible. In Japan, it's not unusual to have an area covered in small rocks and larger stones in place of a green lawn. While it might not have to be mown, it still needs maintenance; don't forget to rake, as it can look messy otherwise. The rake should make patterns in the gravel, so that it appears to flow around the larger stones, just as a river or a stream might. You are trying to emulate or replicate the effect of *kawaakari* (river light) here.

Top Five Walks in Japan

To really experience *shinrin-yoku* in its birthplace, here are some classic walks to add to your bucket list:

1. Nikko

Nikko National Park, and the area around Lake Chuzenji, is famed for its stunning autumnal foliage and dramatic landscapes.

2. Kamakura

I'm completely biased, as I consider Kamakura my cultural hometown when I'm back home in Japan. It's by the sea, *and* is utterly beautiful. The *Daibutsu* trail will lead you past the Giant Buddha (*Daibutsu*) as well as the Zeniarai Benten, a shrine where people go to wash their money in the spring, as it's said to double it.

3. Kumano Kodo

This is the only pilgrimage route other than the Camino de Santiago in Spain designated as a world heritage site. It connects several shrines.

4. Daisetsuzan

A beautiful national park in Hokkaido, Japan's northernmost island. Hokkaido is the least developed of all of Japan's islands, so it's a perfect location if you're looking to immerse yourself in nature.

5. Mount Fuji

Couldn't leave this one off of the list! Mount Fuji is, perhaps, the most iconic Japanese landmark, and one that sits firmly on my bucket list. The sunrise from the summit is said to be incredible.

Going for a walk always seems like such a leisurely activity – one you have to make excuses for, unless you are briskly walking with a destination in mind. It is often reserved as a weekend activity, something to do after a big Sunday lunch, but the benefits go so far beyond that they're almost palpable. Take little breaks, and step outside. Seek out pockets of nature where you can, and incorporate it into your self-care routine – forest bathing can clear your mind in ways that nothing else can.

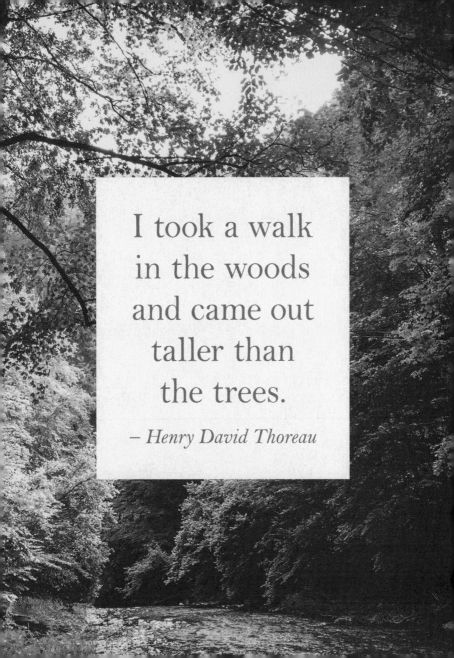

I took a walk
in the woods
and came out
taller than
the trees.

– *Henry David Thoreau*

Ikebana

生け花

The art of flower arranging

Ikebana is the art of flower arranging, but the actual translation of the word is closer to 'giving life to flowers'. Also known as *kado*, or the 'way of flowers', the ancient practice dates back to the seventh century, when flowers were given as offerings in Buddhist temples.

As with almost all art forms, *ikebana* is governed by several schools of thought, each with its own distinct rules and strictly prescribed approaches. Students will practise arrangements through the repetition of different styles, guided by an expert instructor. It is so much more than just putting flowers in a pot or vase – it's a spiritual process, involving a lot of symbolism, and one in which the practitioner becomes closer to nature. Samurai warriors were said to have practised *ikebana* to gain clarity and help them concentrate before battle.

There is a Japanese saying, '*Iwanu ga hana*', which translates as 'not speaking is the flower', in recognition of the virtues of silence, or one who doesn't talk over others. (The closest phrase in English might be 'Silence is golden'.) This conveys an idea of the essence of *ikebana* – it is a gentle, contemplative pastime, which has the benefit of beautifying the home, too.

As an art form, *ikebana* is a silent pursuit, which helps the designer to reflect upon space, balance and their relationship with the natural world. It is meditative, and can help to clear the mind and achieve inner peace. As a result, the final product will often reveal much about the person behind the arrangement, as though they leave a part of themselves in it.

Ikebana arrangements aren't planned in advance, but are discovered or revealed as a result of the ritual process. Beautiful flowers don't necessarily lead to good results, and the arrangement should be approached collaboratively and organically. There's an element of spontaneity and fun, and thinking on your feet in there.

Rather than filling space with flowers, *ikebana* is sculptural – more about finding a sense of balance and harmony in the composition. Flowers and blossoms are contrasted against bare branches, leaves, seedpods and even fruit. Lush flower heads and petals are juxtaposed with withered branches in misshapen clay pots, all of which add to the beauty.

My mother's older sister, Junko, took up *ikebana* as her pastime of choice just before she got married. (Traditionally, many brides-to-be would take up a 'dignified' hobby – either *ikebana* or tea ceremony – to impress their future in-laws.) This is one pastime that's stuck with her, and she still practises the art today.

Ikebana, like the art of calligraphy, plays an integral part in *sado*, or tea ceremony, too. Before a tea ceremony, the guests will admire the *ikebana* arrangement on display, and it becomes a focal feature or point of interest at the event. My grandmother usually has a big floral arrangement by the front door to greet people as they come in; it's also a way to fill and make an alcove a bit more interesting, changing it frequently with the seasons and passing of time.

The Japanese say,
if a flower is beautiful,
it must be cultivated.

– Lester Cole

The Full Bouquet

In many respects, *ikebana* is a little like cooking, which is one of my favourite things to do. I enjoy the process of taking raw ingredients (or, in this case, a few different stems and materials) and transforming them into something completely new. But as with cooking, *ikebana* is not just about the ingredients, but what you do with them. Different chefs will add different seasonings and flavourings to the same dish, and have diverse approaches – and it's the same with *ikebana*: no two arrangements will be the same.

The Three Main Stems

Three core stems form the basis of most arrangements, but additional flowers and plants, known as *jushi*, should accompany them. The three stems represent the relationship between humanity, a higher power and the earth or natural world. They are often placed in the form of a scalene triangle, and the odd number of stems is designed to achieve a minimal, asymmetrical look.

- **Shin.** The *shin* is the longest branch in the arrangement, which symbolically represents heaven. Shin stems or branches should be the most structured, with the ability to stand upright.

- **Soe.** The *soe* is the middle branch in terms of length, and a symbolic representation of man, or humanity. *Soe* should be two-thirds the length of *shin*, as a rough guide.

- **Tai or hikae.** The *tai*, or *hikae*, is the smallest branch, which represents earth and the natural world. *Tai* should be two-thirds the length of *soe*.

These components –
the *shin*, *soe* and *tai* –
should all be measured
in line with your *utsuwa*,
or vase, in a 7:5:3 ratio.
This means that the *shin*
should be the longest
stem (7), the *soe* the
next (5), and the tai the
smallest (3), and they
should be proportional
to each other in this way.
So the longest stem
needs to be around
five times taller than the
smallest stem.

Soe

Shin

Tai or
Hikae

Hanakotoba: The Language of Flowers

Flowers and plants can be charged with meaning beyond the purely aesthetic, and convey an emotion or a feeling without the use of words. *Hanakotoba*, 'the language of flowers', reflects how colours and varieties will have different meanings.

What do different flower varieties symbolise in Japan?

- Bluebell – given in gratitude
- Camellia – waiting or longing
- Daffodil – respect
- Hydrangea – pride
- Iris – good news
- Peony – bravery

Again, thinking about the types of flowers to use as part of your arrangement, and what you want to impart about yourself – whether it's your mood, your frame of mind, any major changes you're going through – is what *ikebana* is all about.

On the whole, white flowers represent death or loss; you probably wouldn't find an all-white bouquet outside of a funeral setting.

Japonisme

Japonisme

Styles of Ikebana

The satisfaction you can gain from practising *ikebana* comes equally from the mental clarity achieved through the process and from the creation of something physically beautiful and striking. True practitioners dedicate years of their lives to perfecting their art, but I find that taking the time to reflect and practise self-care in this way is just as important. Most of us don't have the time or means to devote ourselves to becoming master *ikebana* practitioners, but that doesn't mean we can't enjoy some of the benefits.

For those who want to be as disciplined as possible with the practice, I would suggest going to *Ikebana* International (www.ikebanahq.org/) or finding your local Sogetsu branch (a school of *ikebana*). But for anyone who is just dipping their toes in for the first time, try loosely following one of the five styles below.

—Rikka

The oldest style of *ikebana*, dating back to the fifteenth century, *rikka* is grounded in Buddhism, and the arrangements have a formal, upright style. The seven branches are made to evoke the beauty of a natural landscape, with different stems representing peaks, waterfalls, hills, valleys, towns, shade and sun, perhaps from folklore or mythology.

—Moribana

Moribana translates as 'piled-up flowers'. They are placed in low, shallow containers and often take one of three forms: upright, slanting and water-reflecting. The upright form is the most common, while the slanted form has a softer look, and shows more movement. The water-reflecting form of *moribana* has an element of depth, with the branches and stems playing upon the reflection in the water to complete the effect.

For the most basic style, position *shin*, *soe* and *tai* at the following angles: *shin*, the tallest, should be placed in the back of the *kenzan* (flower frog). If you think about the flower frog as a circle, then it should be at 10°. *Soe* should then be placed at around the 40° point and *tai* at 70°. These angles should be maintained and consistent, whether you are working from the left or the right.

—Nageire

Meaning 'thrown in', *nageire* is one of the only styles that doesn't require a *kenzan*, but only a tall vase. It should look naturally effortless, while still loosely following an asymmetrical triangular structure.

—Seika or shoka

A simplification of *rikka*, but a three-branched asymmetrical style based on *shin*, *soe* and *tai*. There are strict rules and proportions to be adhered to here. The plant material has to be one and a half times the height of the vase, for example, and mountain plants must always go above lowland ones.

—Jiyuka

'Freestyle' or *jiyuka* can be contemporary and abstract, and can also employ non-plant materials (but should still highlight the relationship with nature). Some of these non-organic materials might include wire or netting – again, allow yourself to experiment here.

Ikebana: What You Will Need

- ***Kenzan*, or a flower frog:** a device used to fix the flowers and plants in place in the vase or bowl. It has a flat metal base with metal needles and looks a little like an inverted pin cushion. It's used to spear flowers, so that they stand upright.
- **Scissors:** to trim ends or tidy plants to achieve a simple and minimalist look. Smaller sewing scissors are ideal for some of the more delicate parts of *ikebana*, as you will be working with fragile materials. Have some pruning shears on hand for some of the tougher stems though.
- **Bowl or vase:** this may differ according to whether or not you want to adhere to a specific school or style. Try to keep it simple, as the plants and the form of the arrangement need to speak for themselves. The *nageire* style can use a tall, thin vase, whereas the *moribana* style requires a lower, shallower dish.
- **Plants and flowers:** *ikebana* isn't just about the blooms, but also the sum of its parts. Branches and bamboo in particular can help achieve a minimalist effect. Think carefully about the flowers you use, and what they convey about you. *Ikebana* doesn't have to be an expensive hobby or pastime. I frequent my local flower market most Sunday mornings, and am a massive fan of using dried flowers – they last longer, and there is something very beautiful about petals when they are preserved, giving them an extended life.
- **Floral wire or string:** to hold arrangements in place (especially if yours might also be attempting to defy gravity).
- **A mist bottle:** to keep your arrangements hydrated and looking fresh.

Ikebana: The Process

Ikebana is a transient art, with a significant focus on self-reflection and mindfulness as part of the process. It's about getting in touch with yourself, through the creation of the arrangement, so this isn't the kind of thing you want to do based on a picture you saw on Pinterest. By all means, take a look at different styles to get inspiration, but avoid trying to replicate them. Remember that recreating an arrangement you've seen that was done by someone else defeats the purpose.

Follow these four steps as a guide:

1. Gather

Collect your vessel, equipment and the plants and flowers you plan on using into the environment where your eventual composition will live. This stage is to *ikebana* as *mise en place* is to a chef: it helps you to mentally and physically prepare and organise yourself. Keep the seasons in mind; this is key, as part of the charm of *ikebana* is the interplay between nature and society. Seasonal flowers with blossoms will always work well, and include some green and leafy elements, but also things like branches and twigs. Alluding to the wider *wabi-sabi* philosophy and aesthetic will add an element of authenticity to the process. Note that flower stems should be cut at an angle, to let water in.

2. Place

Place the *kenzan* in the base of the pot, and fill the pot with water. Think about your desired style (I really enjoy the freedom of expression you can get with the *nageire* style, but think about the

Japonisme

design you want to achieve before placing the arrangement). Be conscious of how well the arrangement would travel if you need to move it somewhere else at a later stage.

3. Arrange

Add the stems (around three) in height order, starting with the longest (or *shin*). At this stage, you will need to think about trimming and cutting. Remember that less is always more, and also that you are able to cut a bit more off, but not necessarily add the stem back on. Simplicity and asymmetry are key, but take your surroundings into account too. Look at your arrangements from different angles and distances. Take your time – there is no need to rush – and play with perspective. Get up close and personal, or keep your distance to see how the different stems of the arrangement interact with each other.

4. Finish

Be creative, and not prescriptive. Play with form and design. The key here is to cover the *kenzan*, while still leaving some water visible. Placement of the arrangement, and where it will be displayed, should be kept in mind.

After practising *ikebana*, it is easy to see why generals and other strategists find it therapeutic – it encourages creativity, while presenting a challenge with its constraints. A good arrangement is complex and takes a lot of thought, but the key is not to make it seem that way, but to produce an elegant combination of style and substance.

Tabemono

食べ物

Food

There is no
sincerer love
than the
love of food.

– *George Bernard Shaw*

If my family back in Japan had only one word to describe me, it would probably be *kuishimbo*. It's a tricky one to translate, but it's somewhere between a glutton and a gourmand – someone who gets excited by flavours and food and has a deep appreciation for them. Which is hardly surprising, given that I come from a country where a common saying is *hana yori dango,* meaning 'dumplings over flowers' (referring to someone who prefers substance over style).

I quite like asking people unlikely and hypothetical food-based questions because I think they can reveal a lot about a person's character and personality. For example, 'If you could choose your last meal on earth, what would it be?' Or, one of my favourites: 'If you could only have one cuisine for the rest of your life, what would it be?' (My answer to that is always Japanese food because of the huge range of flavours and textures.)

Researchers have partially attributed the longevity of Japanese people to their diet,[4] which is varied and filled with vegetables, plants and fish. And, luckily for us, it's absolutely delicious, too. There's no other cuisine I crave more, whether it's a big bowl of ramen, gyoza dumplings, a hearty curry or a delicate, succulent piece of sashimi.

Eating, Japanese Style

There is a saying that comes from Okinawa: '*Hara hachi bu*', which means 'Eat until you are 80 per cent full'. Rather than eating until your entire plate is cleared, or you feel stuffed to the gills, eat until you feel comfortably full, and wait a few minutes for your body to process your level of satiety. Then, if you're still not satisfied, go ahead and eat a little more.

My eyes are often much bigger than my stomach, so listening to my body has really helped – because nothing dampens a meal more for me than feeling full to the point of discomfort afterwards.

Listening to your body and eating until you're two-thirds full seems simple enough to do (unless, like me, you've grown up with English grandparents who still have the war-time rationing 'waste not, want not' mentality and insist that you clear your plate entirely). To help with adopting this approach, rather than individually served portions, in Japan (as in a lot of places in Asia), you eat family-style: several different types of dishes, which you tend to serve yourself. You also have lots of little bowls and plates – for soup, rice, a separate one for salad and a small shallow one for dipping.

This makes for a more intimate, communal style of eating, but I also find that I'm able to dish out for myself the exact portion I'd like to eat, which is always an added benefit!

Chopstick Etiquette

Chopsticks are such versatile implements. Once you get the hang of them, using anything else seems like a bit of an effort. The trick to becoming an expert is to simply move the top chopstick, which you hold as you would a pen. It's ok to move the bowl closer to your mouth as well, particularly with a smaller rice bowl.

For chopstick novices, here are my top tips if you're planning a trip to the land of the rising sun:

- **Flip ends to serve.** If you're eating family-style, and you can't see any serving implements, don't stress. This is pretty standard. Simply flip your chopsticks over to the end you won't be putting in your mouth (usually the thicker end) to put food on your plate. It helps to save on washing up, too.

- **No stabbing.** Don't stab your food with your chopsticks, and take care not to leave them standing up in your food. This symbolises death, so make sure you rest them next to a dish (or get yourself some pretty ceramic chopstick rests).

- **Chopsticks should never touch.** Eating something delicious that your dining companion simply has to have a bite of? Don't pass the morsel from your chopsticks to theirs. At Japanese funerals, bone fragments are passed from chopstick to chopstick, so you'd never do this in the context of the dinner table. Pop it on their plate instead (with their permission, of course) or, if you have a super-close relationship, into their mouth directly.

- **Point elsewhere.** Don't use your chopsticks to point at someone or something directly (it's not darts). If you tend to gesture wildly, pop the chopsticks down on your plate, with the thinner ends pointing left.

Bento Boxes

I'm a big fan of the humble bento box, which looks as beautiful as its contents taste and can be traced back to the late Kamakura period, between the late eleventh and early thirteenth centuries. A bento is, essentially, a single-portion takeaway, served in a box, and containing all the elements of a well-balanced meal. While they can also be easily purchased as convenience food, it's a cultural staple, and people spend hours crafting and perfecting them for their loved ones.

The bento box was a key feature of my childhood in Japan, and probably the bane of my mother's life, given how much time can go into making them. They are also great because they can help you save money in the long run. Plus, it meant I always looked forward to my school lunches.

Assembling a bento box

There is a saying that applies so well to bento: '*Nokorimono ni fuku ga aru*' – 'Luck exists in the leftovers!'

—The supplies

Bento boxes work so well because they keep different flavours and textures apart, so you don't end up with one giant, soggy mess. You can buy bento boxes, but you can also repurpose a bog-standard Tupperware by investing in some baking cups or dividers. Sauce containers are also great for storing dressings (to avoid the dreaded limp lettuce) and some colourful toothpicks to hold different pieces together makes it a bit more aesthetically pleasing, too. You can get beautiful lacquered boxes, but they're not as practical as their plastic counterparts, some of which are designed in such a user-friendly way you'd think a team of engineers was hired to create them.

—Keep it colourful

I love taking snaps of my food, much to the chagrin of my friends, and am a big fan of a beautiful plate. When you're packing a bento, think of different colours you can include to make it look as good as it tastes. Think red cabbage instead of green, throw in some radish and add different fruits and vegetables to shake things up a little.

—The ratio

Typically, bento boxes are:

- Four parts carbohydrate (typically rice or noodles, but you could also have quinoa, potato salad, whatever you've got going on in the fridge).
- Two parts vegetable (something like spinach with a sesame dressing, green beans, bean sprouts; if you like a bit of crunch, you can pack the dressing in a separate container to keep it crisp, and avoid the dreaded lunchbox wilt).
- One part protein (this might be chicken, fish, sausages or a tofu-based dish; again, raid the fridge for leftovers and think creatively).
- One part fruit (oranges work well, as do grapes, blueberries and strawberries; I always prefer whole apples, rather than cutting slices and adding lemon to them, but they are harder to transport in a little bento box).

Keep all of the above component parts separate from each other (again, no one likes soggy *karaage* fried chicken or garlicky kiwi fruit).

Comfort Food, the Japanese Way

If using chopsticks isn't your thing, then a good alternative to a bento box might be something you can grab on the go, like *onigiri*. There's something very satisfying and comforting about shaping the warm rice by hand – but if you're feeling lazy, you can always buy moulds to get the perfect shape too.

Onigiri rice balls

As much as I like taking long lunch breaks, real life gets in the way. I absolutely love *onigiri* for lunches on the go – triangular rice balls covered in *nori* (roasted seaweed) that can be filled with something delicious, like pickled plum, cooked salmon or tuna mayonnaise.

Serves 1

70g short-grain rice
pinch of salt
filling of your choice (savoury – e.g. pickled *umeboshi* plum, cooked
    salmon, tuna mayonnaise)
¼ sheet *nori* seaweed

1. Cook the rice in salted water and wait for it to cool slightly, until it's comfortable enough to handle.
2. With your hands, mould it gently into the shape of a triangle, and make a slight indentation in the centre using the pad of your thumb.
3. Spoon a little of your desired filling into the middle, and then reshape the *onigiri*, so that the rice covers the filling completely.
4. Wrap some *nori* around the *onigiri* rice ball and tuck in.

Yaki onigiri (grilled rice balls)

These are my weakness. They are perfect if you want to jazz up your *onigiri*.

Serves 1

1 *onigiri*
1 tbsp soy sauce

1. Take your *onigiri* and pop it in a lightly oiled oven pan, grilling it for 5 minutes on each side.
2. Using a pastry brush, coat each side with a little soy sauce, and return to the pan for a couple of minutes on each side. It'll be crispy on the outside, but light and fluffy on the inside, and the extra soy sauce gives it a further boost of umami flavour.

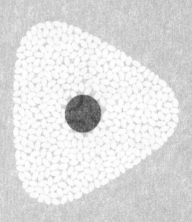

RED MISO

WHITE MISO

NATTO

Fermented Foods

The traditional Japanese diet is full of fermented foods. The probiotics gained from eating these are great for your digestive health, too. I really love *tsukemono* (pickled vegetables) and *umeboshi* (pickled plums), but in terms of my top five essentials, these are the ones to beat:

1. Natto

Natto is the Japanese equivalent of Marmite, meaning you either love it or hate it. These fermented soybeans have quite a strong odour, not dissimilar to a strong cheese, and are typically eaten in the morning with rice, soy sauce and *karashi* (Japanese mustard). The small, densely packed brown soybeans take on a sticky consistency when stirred or activated by the addition of liquid (in this case, soy sauce and Japanese mustard).

My love of *natto* definitely comes from the fact that I grew up eating it, and ties into the feeling of *natsukashii*, or the nostalgic fondness I have for it. I don't know many people who have tried it for the first time in adulthood who like it. It's definitely an acquired taste.

2. Miso

I love miso so much I named my cat after it. This fermented soybean paste makes my favourite soup, but also works great in stews (just add a teaspoon if you need more flavour), dressings and glazes. You can find some tasty recipes using miso on pages 157 and 158.

T
A
B
E
M
O
N
O

3. Tofu

Tofu, also known as soybean curd, is full of protein and iron and, when prepared correctly, it is one of my favourite foods. Made by pressing coagulating soy milk into blocks, tofu is really subtle and mild in flavour, and takes on the flavours of whatever it is served with.

I love tofu in miso soup, but *agedashi* tofu (deep-fried tofu with a *tsuyu* sauce made from *dashi*, mirin and soy sauce) is seriously delicious. Check out the recipe on page 154.

4. Soy sauce

Another one of my favourite hypothetical food-based questions is 'If you could only have one condiment for the rest of your life, what would it be?' Mine is always soy sauce. I put it in everything: chilli, Bolognese, roast chicken . . . It is, in my opinion, the most versatile sauce out there – salty perfection in a bottle!

There are numerous different types of soy sauces. Here's my quick guide:

• **Dark soy sauce – *koikuchi*.** The most popular variety of soy sauce, *koikuchi* (meaning 'dark mouth') is made with equal parts soybean and wheat. This is the kind you'd probably find available at your local supermarket.

• **Light soy sauce – *usukuchi*.** Saltier than *koikuchi*, *usukuchi* ('light mouth') is a lighter variety and not as strongly fermented. It originates from the Kansai region of Japan.

- **Wheat-free soy sauce – *tamari*.** *Tamari* is made using no wheat, so if you've ever bought gluten-free soy sauce, it's most definitely tamari. It's more dense than *koikuchi*, but has a very similar flavour.

- **White soy sauce – *shiro shoyu*.** In contrast to *tamari*, s*hiro shoyu* is made using mostly wheat, and very little of the soybean. Because the hue is so pale, it's used for light soups and broths, as well as dishes like a savoury egg custard (*chawanmushi*).

- **Low-salt soy sauce – *genen shoyu*.** One for those who are trying to limit their salt intake, this is made using a similar process to *koikuchi*, while reducing the amount of salt.

- **Whole-bean soy sauce – *marudaizu shoyu*.** This is considered to be a more premium version, as it uses whole soybeans, and has a more complex flavour as a result. It is usually served with sushi.

5. Katsuobushi

Katsuobushi, also known as bonito flakes, are dried, fermented and smoked tuna flakes. They are often used as one of the main components of *dashi*, the stock that forms the basis of most Japanese dishes. If you use *katsuobushi* flakes to make a stock, be sure to keep them afterwards. You can then pop them in a frying pan with a little sesame oil and add some sesame seeds and seaweed to lightly toast and dry the flakes up again. They will keep for a few months in the fridge and work perfectly as *furikake*, or flavoured rice seasoning. Simply sprinkle it over the top of a bowl of plain steamed rice to give it some flavour, or stir it in well to incorporate it into your *onigiri* rice balls. Delicious!

Agedashi tofu

This is served hot, and the crispy outside, contrasting with the soft centre, is delicious – not dissimilar to the experience of eating mozzarella sticks. The umami flavour from the *dashi* really elevates it.

Serves 2

300g firm tofu
salt
120ml *dashi* stock
2 tsp soy sauce
1 tsp mirin
1 tsp sugar
50g potato starch
vegetable oil, for deep-frying
spring onions, to serve

1. Cut the tofu into even pieces, around 2–3cm each. Place the pieces on a wire rack, and salt them generously – the salt will help to draw the water out of the tofu, which will make it easier to fry them without losing their shape. Set aside for 10 minutes.
2. Meanwhile, get the *tsuyu* sauce ready. Combine the *dashi* stock, soy sauce, mirin and sugar in a saucepan, place on a high heat and bring to the boil. Once it's reached a rolling boil, turn the heat down and let it simmer.
3. With a paper towel, gently wipe the excess salt off of the tofu pieces, then coat them evenly with the potato starch.

4. Heat a generous amount of oil in a saucepan – you want the pieces to be evenly cooked through.
5. Deep-fry the tofu pieces until they puff, but make sure they don't take on too much colour.
6. Serve the tofu in a small bowl, with some *tsuyu* sauce and a few spring onions sliced diagonally and scattered over the top.

Black cod with miso

People are always surprised at how simple it really is to make black cod with a miso marinade – it does require some advanced planning and prep, but is the perfect dinner-party feast. If you don't have black cod, you can use any kind of oily fish, like salmon.

Serves 1

120g black cod fillet
salt
100g white miso (shiro miso) paste
25g sugar
2 tsp mirin
2 tsp *sake*

1. Salt the black cod to draw out excess moisture, and leave it to stand for a couple of hours. With a clean paper towel, wipe off the excess salt.
2. In a saucepan, heat through the miso, sugar, mirin and *sake* on a low heat, until the sugar has dissolved completely.
3. Pour the marinade into a baking tray, and place the fillets in it, stirring to coat all sides. Leave it to marinate for about 24 to 48 hours in the fridge, so the cod fillets take on some colour (a light brown hue) and flavour.
4. Preheat the oven to 220°C. With your fingers, wipe off the excess marinade from the fish. If you leave too much of this on, you run the risk of it burning and crusting on the fillet, which isn't ideal as it's not cheap!
5. Bake the fish, skin-side up, for about 10 minutes, or until browned and caramelised slightly. Serve with steamed rice and a salad.

Miso aubergine

Miso is a great source of protein and B vitamins, and can, reportedly, help lower cholesterol and ease digestion. One of my favourite side dishes, miso aubergine (*nasu dengaku*) works well as an accompaniment to poached fish, or even just on its own with a bowl of plain rice.

Serves 4

2 aubergines
salt
vegetable oil, for brushing
100g miso paste
3 tsp sugar
4 tbsp mirin
sesame seeds, to serve

1. Preheat the oven to 200°C.
2. Cut the aubergines in half, and leave to soak for 10 minutes in a bowl of salted water. I find this helps to reduce bitterness.
3. Drain the water, and score the aubergines, brushing each side generously with some oil.
4. Place the aubergines on a baking tray lined with foil, and roast for 10 minutes, scored-side up. Then turn them over and roast them for a further 5 minutes, bottom-side up.

5. While the aubergines are roasting, mix the remaining ingredients in a saucepan to make the glaze and heat until simmering gently. Let it reduce slightly, adding water, if necessary, to ensure it doesn't reduce too much and to avoid burning. It should be the colour and texture of a buttery caramel.

6. Once the aubergines are cooked through, take them out of the oven and cover with the glaze. Place them under a hot grill for a couple of minutes before serving, sprinkled with sesame seeds.

Sushi

I have several friends who, upon first meeting me, claimed not to be fans of sushi. But I've managed to convince most of them over time, and they have become firm converts. Sushi is a bit like seeing a well-known piece of art for the first time – you won't really get what the big deal is or understand it until you've experienced it properly first-hand. The key is finding a good place – not all hamburgers are created equal, and the same goes for sushi. Quality is key.

For any sceptics out there, I challenge you to watch my favourite film – *Jiro Dreams of Sushi* – and not want to lick your screen after. It is a visual masterpiece, and will have you itching to make your own!

Making sushi

Making sushi doesn't really feel like cooking to me – it's more akin to arts and crafts. It does require some assembly, but is a lot simpler than you might think. The flavourings are straightforward, but getting the ingredients right is key. For example, the rice has to be short-grain (long-grain or basmati will simply fall apart as they're not sticky enough). And as for the fish, if you're not able to get your hands on premium- or sushi-quality fish, I would stick with a vegetarian option – it'll be a nicer experience than attempting it with lower-quality fish that might not be as fresh.

Serves 4
150g short-grain sushi rice
4 sheets *nori* seaweed, lightly toasted

For the rice seasoning
1 packet Sushi no ko (powdered sushi vinegar)
    or 3 tbsp rice vinegar
3 tbsp caster sugar
2 tsp table salt

For the fillings
around 220g of any of the below:
premium-grade salmon sashimi
premium-grade tuna sashimi
½ cucumber, peeled and cut into batons
100g crab stick
½ avocado, cut into slivers

Optional

soy sauce

wasabi

pickled ginger

Equipment

metal tray

bamboo sushi mat

bowl of water

cling film

a sharp knife

1. Cook the sushi rice using your preferred method – most homes in Japan will have an electric rice cooker as a standard household staple (so much so that it was the first appliance my dad bought for me when I went off to university). If you don't have a rice cooker, then the stove method is fine – cook until light and fluffy by keeping the lid on after the water boils.

2. Mix all the rice-seasoning ingredients in a bowl (if you are using rice vinegar, make sure the granules have dissolved). Spread the rice out onto the metal tray, and stir the seasoning mixture into it. Leave to cool slightly or until the rice can be handled comfortably (blood temperature). If you're feeling impatient, you can always fan your rice to cool it down. If you're really getting hungry, you can even use your hairdryer on the cool setting!

3. Giving yourself plenty of space to manoeuvre, lay the bamboo sushi mat out flat, and place a roasted nori seaweed sheet on top. Keep your bowl of water near by – you'll need this to dampen your hands throughout the process, to prevent the rice from sticking to you instead of the surface.

4. Take a look at the seaweed sheet, and mentally divide it into four quarters or panels. Cover three quarters of the sheet with a thin, even layer of rice, keeping the quarter nearest to you free.

5. Leaving a gap of about a centimetre of rice, put your desired fillings in the quarter closest to your body, going across the mat horizontally. It's always tempting to pack a lot of filling in, but you want it to look neat and not spill out too much, so don't get too carried away.

6. Pick up the edge of the mat, and slowly roll it over onto itself, compressing lightly along the way – just enough to encourage the roll to come together, without squishing it or applying too much pressure. Keep rolling the mat forward until you reach the end – the roll should have come together.

7. Using a sharp, slightly moistened knife, trim the ends so they look neat and even. If you're not serving immediately, then wrap the maki roll in a little cling film. Serve with a side of soy sauce, wasabi and pickled ginger, if desired.

Eating Sushi

- You usually eat sushi with your hands, so make sure they are clean. Most places will provide a hot towel for this purpose.
- If you can, try and sit up at the counter by the sushi chef and get his or her recommendations.
- Pour a little bit of soy sauce into a dipping bowl. Don't dip the rice in, but flip the sushi over and lightly coat the fish with the sauce – this will prevent it from falling apart.
- To wasabi or not to wasabi… Interestingly, wasabi first accompanied sushi dishes when refrigeration wasn't widely available, to kill off any bacteria that might have been in the fish, but has since become a key component of this cuisine. At a traditional restaurant, the chef will have already seasoned the sushi, depending on the type of fish. But, as they say, different strokes for different folks, and some like the extra heat more than others. You can try adding a little wasabi to your soy sauce to flavour it, and add depth and complexity, without letting it become too overpowering.
- Eat the sushi in one bite, and chew slowly. It's all about appreciating the flavours, and the balance in textures; it's not about scoffing it all down.
- Cleanse the palate with a bit of ginger between pieces, particularly different types of fish.

Japonisme

The Starring Roll

There are lots of different ways to prepare sushi, and making sure
you don't get your rolls mixed up is always handy. 'Sushi' refers to
raw fish that has rice as a base, whereas 'sashimi' is without rice.

- **Maki:** *nori* seaweed surrounds the rice seasoned with vinegar, with
  a filling in the centre.

- **Uramaki:** not strictly traditional, *uramaki*, or the inside-out roll, is
  when the rice is on the outside, surrounding the *nori* seaweed and
  filling. California rolls (avocado and crab) are commonly served in
  this style, usually with a sprinkling of sesame seeds coating the roll
  as well.

- **Nigiri:** hand-pressed sushi, where a cylindrical roll of rice has a
  topping (or *neta*) placed over it, as though it's been tucked under
  a blanket.

- **Temaki:** a hand roll, which slightly resembles an ice-cream cone in
  shape, with a sheet of *nori* seaweed wrapped around the rice and
  filling. I don't know why, but I love eating salmon *temaki* the best. I
  think it's something about the creaminess of the salmon flesh that
  works so well eaten in this way.

- **Chirashi:** *chirashizushi*, or scattered sushi, is served in a bowl,
  which is topped with raw fish and vegetable garnishes. It was my
  mom's go-to dish for school picnics because it's quick and easy to
  prepare, and usually eaten in March for *hinamatsuri*, or Girls' Day.

Ramen

Every time my sister and I visit Japan, particularly in the summer, we insist on going to our favourite grimy, hole-in-the-wall ramen bar in a sleepy neighbourhood near where my aunt and cousins used to live. Even when a few years have passed, they always remember us in there, and incorporating our ramen pilgrimage into our schedule has become standard family practice. There is nothing more satisfying than that combination of a salty broth, tender pork and crunchy bamboo shoots – my mouth waters whenever I think about it.

Eating Ramen Like a Local

A few words to the wise for when you're eating ramen:

- Ramen is a salty dish, so no need to try and finish all of the broth – you'll need a lot of water afterwards!
- Let them hear your appreciation. Audible slurping is a good thing. Don't overdo it, though, as your appreciation and enjoyment should be sincere and not exaggerated.
- Ramen is the kind of dish you tend to eat quickly, and on the go. It doesn't lend itself to being savoured over a long time, as the noodles will go soggy and disintegrate. Make haste!

Ramen at Home

Ramen is the ultimate comfort food for me. There's something about being hunched over a steaming bowl of the delicious, umami-filled savoury broth that makes me feel so cosy, especially in the winter.

—Embellishing instant ramen

For some, instant noodles might conjure up images of lazy, spotty teenagers hankering after an afternoon snack. In Japan, however, packets of instant ramen are pretty commonplace. There is even a whole museum devoted to the humble cup noodle. So love it or hate it, it's a staple of Japanese cuisine – to the extent that a Michelin-star-awarded ramen restaurant has released its own variety that can be bought in supermarkets throughout Japan. It's the Nakiryu Dan Dan Noodle, and has had rave reviews.

Just because it's instant, though, doesn't mean it has to feel grimy. By using packets of instant noodles in clever ways, you can make a tasty and delicious meal without any guilt or embarrassment. Here are my top tips for making a packet of instant noodles respectable:

1. **Use fresh vegetables.** 'See, it's healthy!' you'll be able to claim. Once your family or guests see the addition of spinach leaves, mangetout, bamboo shoots, bean sprouts and sliced spring onion, they'll have a tough time disputing that.

2. **Pack in the protein.** Still got that chicken breast from your roast dinner on Sunday? Chuck it in. Leftover ham slices? Tear them up and sprinkle them on top. Adding in a bit of protein will make it look (and taste) like a proper hearty meal, rather than the carb fest it might otherwise be.

3. **Add some eggs.** I love poaching an egg in the broth as I heat it to soften the noodles through – there is something so decadent and satisfying about poking the poached egg, and letting the yolk enrich the broth as you tuck in. If you're not a confident poacher of eggs, a boiled one would work, too. A soft-boiled egg is highly recommended – once you've cooked it to your preference, blanch the egg, peel off the shell and slice across, so the beautiful colour of the yolk can be seen in contrast with the brown broth and colourful vegetables.

4. **Season well.** I like a bit of heat, so I tend to add a good crack of freshly ground pepper and some shichimi, or Japanese seven-spice powder. I also like to add a splash of my favourite brand of soy sauce or even a teaspoon of miso. It's all dependent on your taste, but make it your own!

Japonisme

Ramen from scratch

For some, ramen might be considered fast food, but making it by hand is certainly not. A delicious bowl of ramen takes time and a lot of TLC. There is something incredibly satisfying about watching all the components come together – and making it yourself means you can get your noodles just the way you like them.

—The noodles

Making ramen noodles isn't something most people do all the time. It's a bit like the way most of us think of fresh pasta: why make it from scratch when you can get it from the shops? Fresh ramen noodles (i.e. not the dehydrated variety you get with instant) can readily be bought at a supermarket, so I only started making my own a year or so ago. It is very similar to the way fresh pasta is made – and, as with pasta, those who do make their own noodles swear by it.

You will need a pasta machine on the spaghetti setting. And you'll also need a strong pasta flour – the '00' variety, which has a high protein content and is finely milled. The flour here is extremely important. Don't substitute it for all-purpose – that's one compromise you don't want to make, especially when you're going to so much effort.

Serves 4
6g bicarbonate of soda
4g salt
90ml hot water
110ml room-temperature water
400g '00' pasta flour
30g cornflour

1. Mix the bicarbonate of soda and salt in a small jug with the hot water and stir until they have dissolved completely, before adding the room-temperature water.

2. In a large bowl, sift the flour before adding the liquid from the jug. Using a spatula, mix this until flakes start to form – if it feels too watery, add a little more flour, and if it's a little too dehydrated, add a bit more liquid.

3. Lightly dust your surface with a little of the cornflour, before returning to your bowl. Bring the dough together, and remove it from the bowl before beginning to work it on the floured surface. You want to knead it until the dough isn't too sticky, and springs back slightly.

4. Form the dough into a ball and wrap it with cling film. Pop it in the fridge for around half an hour or so.

5. Remove the dough from the fridge, and knead again until smooth, silky and elastic. Divide into four equally sized balls – these will be the portions of noodles per person.

6. Flour the surface again, to prevent any sticking, before rolling your dough through the pasta machine. Following the manufacturer's instructions, roll the dough through, starting with the machine on its widest setting. Roll the dough through each setting twice, changing the setting, so the dough becomes thinner and thinner as you progress.

7. Take your thin noodle sheet and, using the spaghetti-cutting attachment, cut into thin ribbons. Leave to dry (without tangling) for another half an hour.

8. Just before your broth is ready, bring a saucepan of salted water to a rapidly rolling boil before turning down to a simmer. Place the noodles in a small sieve, and lower them gently into the

pan, cooking for about 3 minutes. Taste to test the texture, but remember that the noodles will continue cooking in the hot broth, so remove them from the pan when just al dente.

9. Once you've poured your broth into bowls, pop the noodles in before finishing with pork, eggs, bamboo shoots or any of the toppings listed on page 179.

—The broth

The broth is what gives a bowl of ramen its depth of flavour. There are many different types of broths, depending on the region, but most common are the shoyu-based (my personal favourite) and the miso-based ones.

The broth is made from one part concentrate and two parts stock.

For the concentrate:

• Shoyu ramen
This gives a deep and savoury flavour to the broth. Combine 1 tsp sesame oil, 1 tbsp dark soy sauce, 1 tbsp oyster sauce and ½ tsp each of rice vinegar and salt.

• Miso ramen
The miso soybean paste gives the dish a nuttier and more earthy flavour than the shoyu, and is a little sweeter, too. Combine 1½ tbsp miso paste, ½ tbsp soy sauce, ¼ tbsp salt and 1 tsp sugar.

For the stock:

The broth is two-thirds stock, so if you've put in the effort and the time to make the noodles and the concentrate, this isn't something you'll want to cut corners on. This is a recipe for a *tonkotsu* stock. While time-consuming, it is delicious – it involves boiling down pork bones for hours and skimming off any scum that rises to the surface.

1.5kg pork bones
750g chicken carcasses
2 large onions, diced
1 leek, sliced
1 garlic bulb, crushed
200g mushrooms, sliced

1. Place the pork bones and chicken carcasses into a large stock pot and cover with cold water. Pop a lid on, place over a high heat and bring to a rolling boil.

2. Once the stock has reached a rolling boil, drain the pot, and wipe any coagulated blood off of the bones, rinsing them in cold water.

3. Making sure the stock pot is clean, put the bones back in and add the remaining ingredients. Add water to cover by more than a centimetre or two, place on a high heat and bring to the boil again.

4. Once the stock has boiled, turn the heat down, so it is barely simmering, and leave for 6–12 hours. I like to pop mine in my slow cooker, and then it can be left for longer. Check on it periodically to skim off any fat and scum that have risen to the surface.

5. At the end of the cooking time, you should have a cloudy stock – drain well before adding to your desired ramen concentrate.

Note: A good-quality chicken stock will work well, too. Simply add 600ml stock to the concentrate, before adding the noodles and various toppings.

—The toppings
Traditional toppings include slivers of char siu pork, egg, bamboo shoots, sesame seeds, eggs, seaweed and spring onion.

Japanese Foodisms

The Japanese language has a few words and expressions that are used solely around the dinner table, or any time you are about to eat.

—Goshisousama

Before digging into a meal in Japan, people always say *itadakimasu*, which literally translates as 'I humbly receive', and end it with *goshisousama*, meaning, 'That was a feast'. It's a way of showing appreciation to the host or chef for feeding you.

—Kuidaore

Another word that reveals the deep love and appreciation for good food in Japan is *kuidaore,* which means eating until the point of bankruptcy, or spending all of your money on food. The Japanese love a good food trend – people will willingly queue up to get their hands on the latest food fad, whatever it might be – and spending money on good food and eating well is definitely a common theme.

—Oishii

When I was a little girl I used to tell my mother that I would grow up to be one of the girls on Japanese morning TV, who would travel around the country sampling various delicacies and saying '*Oishii*'! *Oishii* means delicious – and if you hear it said outside a restaurant, then it's probably worth popping in.

I firmly believe that nourishing food is transformative, and can transcend language and cultural barriers. Eating well is living well – and enjoying your food can give so much pleasure. Seek quality over quantity and, when in doubt, go for slow. Good things are worth the wait, and food is one of them – whether it's simmering a broth for hours to achieve the perfect ramen base, the time it takes for the soybean to ferment into its delicious, umami-rich form or the length of time needed for produce to grow. Savour the moment when eating; make sure you can appreciate taking food in and relish the flavours, as well as the company of your dining companions.

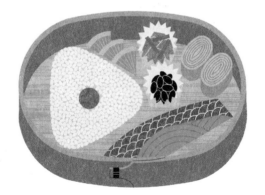

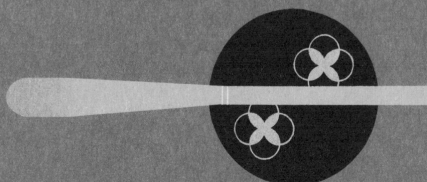

Ocha

お茶

Tea

If a man has no tea
in him, he is incapable
of understanding
truth and beauty.

— *Japanese proverb*

My English and Japanese relatives don't have much in common, but the sound of a boiling kettle has always been a constant in my life – we are all big tea drinkers.

The Japanese word for the colour brown is *cha-iro*, which literally means 'colour of tea'. This should give you an indication of just how passionate we are about the stuff. There are so many varieties of tea in Japan – it is so much more than just matcha, with many different types suited for different seasons and different occasions.

It's not uncommon for people to take their favourite cup with them when they are out and about. And with good reason, too, as I can't remember a time I've had a truly good cup of tea out of a plastic takeaway cup! The most delicious tea comes from being paid special attention and this extends to what it's served in as well.

Tea is serious business, folks! So why don't you go and pop the kettle on?

Sado – Tea Ceremony

Sado (or *chado*), also known as 'The Way of the Tea', is the ceremonial presentation of a powdered green tea called matcha. The performance itself is referred to as *otemae*, and becoming a practitioner takes a lot of time and dedication.

My Aunt Taeko has spent around twenty-three years perfecting the art. Chatting to her recently, I asked about her motivation, given how much of herself she has invested in tea ceremony. She is a senior executive at a major advertising agency, and a mother of two – didn't she already have enough on her plate?

Taeko explained that she turned to tea because she felt her work and home life were passing by too quickly. Through *sado*, she said, she gave herself a day a week to reflect mentally and relax. For her, tea ceremony helped the day-to-day pressures of work and family drift away, allowing her to engage with the changing seasons in a more natural way, rather than thinking about deadlines, the end of financial years or whatever she had to achieve before the next quarter. She told me:

'When I'm at work, there's always an element of competition, and it can sometimes feel like a race. You have to make compromises, or work with people you don't want to. But when I'm performing tea ceremony, I forget about all of that. It helps me to realise that human beings are just a part of nature, and the bigger picture, and helps me put things into perspective.'

Japonisme

Another important part of the process for her was connecting with Japanese culture, and spiritual culture in particular, and centring herself.

There are two types of ceremony – *chaji* and *chakai*. *Chaji* is the full-length, formal, bells-and-whistles version, and can take up to four hours, including a full meal. A *chakai* is more of an informal gathering, with lighter refreshments and a less rigid format. Guests also have prescribed roles in Japanese tea ceremonies, both formal and informal.

The Principles of Tea

Sado is founded on four key principles, attributed to the sixteenth-century tea master Sen Rikyu. Practitioners of tea ceremony aim not only to apply these principles in the context of the tea ceremony, but also to integrate them into their daily lives outside of the tearoom. They are as follows:

1. Wa – harmony
Living harmoniously with each other, but also with nature – being movable, flexible and changeable.

2. Kei – respect
Having respect for the process and the ceremony, but also for each other, as well as the implements and equipment, through taking care and a muted, unassuming pride in the practice.

3. Sei – purity
Purity, in this instance, refers to cleanliness and orderliness, but also to being authentic, clear and transparent – a purity of mind and spirit.

4. Jaku – tranquillity

This cannot be attained without putting the other principles into practice, but it's more about an elevation of the mind or a specific state of mindfulness. This is probably the hardest to learn, as it requires a high level of discipline to embody tranquillity both within and outside of your practice.

These four principles can definitely have wider application outside of tea ceremony: we could all learn from living harmoniously, respectfully and having a bit more organisation in our lives in order to achieve tranquillity and contentment.

Koicha and Usucha – Thick and Thin Teas

Matcha is prepared in two different ways during a tea ceremony: *koicha* (thick tea) and *usucha* (thin tea).

—Koicha

This is offered first, and the cup is shared among three guests, who take three sips each before passing it on (after wiping the rim with hemp cloth or *kaishi* paper – a folded piece of paper stashed in your kimono for hygiene purposes). It requires around three times more tea than *usucha*, and is gently whisked into the cup in order to ensure a smooth blend.

—Usucha

The thinner tea is whisked or whipped into the hot water, and each guest will drink from their own individual cup.

Equipment

No tea ceremony is complete without the proper gear (*chadogu*). You should invest quite a bit in your *chadogu* and like a chef and their knives, you become quite familiar and intimate with your tools.

- **Cha-ire:** This is a tea caddy with a lid, usually made out of ceramic. The tea is stored in and dispensed from it. The *cha-ire* is filled before the tea ceremony, and when it is being performed the guests would see you measuring out from it.

- **Chasen:** The *chasen* whisk is made from bamboo, and is damaged often, so it is frequently replaced. Because it is delicate, it needs to be handled appropriately – you wouldn't use it to scramble your eggs! The movements in *sado* are all soft, deliberate and gentle, never forced.

- **Chakin:** This is a white hemp cloth used to wipe down the rim of the bowl after a guest has taken a sip of their tea.

- **Chawan:** The tea cup or bowl is the most important element of the tea ceremony. You tend to have shallow bowls in the summer, to encourage the tea to cool, and deeper ones in the winter for the opposite effect. Chipped and imperfect cups are prized, their flaws being points of interest, admired by the guests. (Broken cups are repaired through *kintsugi* – mending with gold – see pages 78–83.)

- **Chasaku:** The tea scoop, also known as *chashaku*, is carved from a single piece of a material like ivory or bamboo, and is used to scoop the tea from the caddy into the cup.

Hosting Your Own Tea Ceremony

Tempted to host your own tea ceremony at home? Here are some top tips to keep in mind:

Location, Location, Location

Tea ceremonies are usually performed in special tearooms, known as *chashitsu*. These are lined with tatami floor mats, and you should avoid stepping on the places where they join up. You'll be sitting *seiza*-style, on your knees on the ground. At home, you might think about moving furniture around to create a sense of space, adding floor cushions for your guests. Or you could also consider hosting a *nodate* – a tea ceremony outside, like a picnic.

Setting the Scene

For an authentic tea ceremony, you need to have the following in the room:

- **Calligraphy:** in the form of a hanging scroll on the wall of the room. It should be topical, relating to the season or theme of the gathering. (A common theme running through all of these ancient customs and art forms is being reminded of the time of year.)
- **Food:** any excuse for some food. A *kaiseki* (Japanese meal with multiple courses, similar to haute cuisine) is served on individual lacquered tables, and is seasonal, usually adorned with edible flowers and herbs. It needs to be beautifully presented, of course.
- **Flowers:** these are everywhere! There is a special style of *ikebana* flower arrangement, known as *chabana*, created in a *nageire* style (see page 128). The flowers need to be seasonal, but minimalist and stripped down – one or two stems at most – so as not to overpower, either through smell (which might detract from the experience of tea and disturb the flavours and palate) or visually (away from the ceremony itself).

Dress Code

The host will always wear a kimono, which is as practical as it is beautiful. Kimonos have many places to stash necessary items, like fans – say, in the *obi* (belt) or in the long sleeves.

If, as a guest, you don't have a kimono, then dress formally, but not over the top. The focus here is on the tea and the ceremony, not the fashion. You don't want to detract from the practice by wearing something showy or ostentatious.

MATCHA

GENMAICHA

SENCHASOH
IPPUKU ICHIHUKU
MATSUE SHIRO NO SHIRO

御抹茶・松江城の白

一服一福

KUKICHA

HOJICHA

SENCHA

Japanese Tea Varieties: A Guide

When most people think of Japanese tea, matcha is the most likely variety to spring to mind. Matcha mania has spread all over the place, with new cafés popping up everywhere, and you can get matcha lattes at most high-street coffee bars now.

But there are so many different varieties of Japanese teas beyond just matcha to be explored. Here is a handy guide on which type of tea to drink and when.

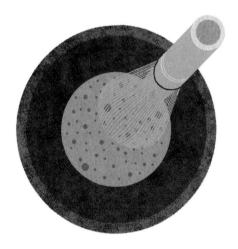

—Sencha Japanese tea

When someone asks for *ocha*, they are usually referring to *sencha*, which is the most common green tea. It's also referred to as *nihoncha*, which literally means 'Japanese tea'. In fact, 80 per cent of the tea produced in Japan is of the sencha variety. It is the perfect accompaniment to a meal, especially dishes like tempura or seafood, as it has a fairly mild flavour. *Sencha* is a steamed tea, and needs to be brewed in something that allows the leaves to expand, so the flavour can be infused into the water properly.

The perfect temperature to brew *sencha* is around 75°C, in order to achieve the perfect mellow flavour and colour, which is a green-tinged gold. If the water is too hot, you run the risk of it going too sharp, which makes it overly bitter, sharp and acidic. You can get a few steeps out of the same leaves, and I usually find the third steep to be the tastiest. It's incredibly moreish. I've now got my housemate hooked on it (she's on about three cups a day).

—Genmaicha (popcorn) rice tea

Genmaicha is a blend of *bancha*, which is a lower-grade version of *sencha*, along with roasted rice (*genmai*). It's sometimes called popcorn tea, because the rice can pop when it's being made, just as corn does. It's got quite a nutty flavour and a yellow colour. It's the perfect tea for settling your stomach if you're not feeling like your usual self.

—Hojicha roasted tea

Hojicha is my Japanese grandmother, Motoko's (or Baba's), favourite tea. It's almost caffeine-free, so it's perfect for after dinner. It's roasted, and has an aroma not dissimilar to coffee, with a reddish-brown hue. This is my favourite tea, too.

—Kukicha (twig) tea

Also known as twig tea, *kukicha* is unusual because it incorporates the stems, stalks and twigs that are usually discarded. It's sweeter and creamier than other teas and can be brewed multiple times. Unlike the other Japanese teas featured here, it's not as astringent, so if you are a fan of a milder tea, this might be the one for you.

—Matcha powdered green tea

Matcha tea refers to a finely ground verdant green tea powder, and can be categorised into three grades: ceremonial (for tea ceremonies), premium (for everyday use) and culinary (for cooking). Its deep green colour makes it a popular ingredient for dyeing food.

Matcha has a slightly bitter taste, so it's a great accompaniment to sweet dishes and desserts, as it contrasts with and complements them so well. My personal favourite way to have matcha is in ice cream, but you can also have it in pastries, lattes and even blended into smoothies.

—Mugicha barley tea

To me, *mugicha* tastes like going on holiday. It's a barley tea, and you usually have it cold, in the summer. It's incredibly refreshing, but has quite a bitter taste. While people do drink it hot, it is the go-to Japanese summer thirst quencher, so it can be purchased really easily in tea bags that don't require boiling. You simply pop a *mugicha* tea bag into a jug of cold water, and leave it to steep in the fridge while it infuses with flavour.

Ocha zuke (tea-topped rice)

Sencha is incredibly versatile, and I was extremely grateful for it back in my student days when I was on a budget and living in halls. *Ocha zuke*, or tea-topped rice, is a really common meal for students, for a quick snack or even if you need to cure a hangover. It's a fantastic way of using leftovers, too. You can experiment with different toppings, but my favourites include *umeboshi* (pickled plums) or salmon flakes.

Serves 1

steamed white short-grain rice (about 120g)
boiled *sencha* (about 175ml)
1 thinly sliced *nori* seaweed sheet, toasted

Suggested toppings

cooked salmon
sea bream
sesame seeds
spring onions, thinly sliced
wasabi
Japanese rice crackers, crushed
umeboshi (pickled plums)
soy sauce
pollock roe

1. Put the warm, cooked rice in a small rice bowl, and cover with your desired toppings. I personally love flaking some leftover salmon over it, along with spring onions, toasted *nori* seaweed, some crushed Japanese rice crackers (called *bubu arare*, if you can get your hands on them at all) and a little wasabi for some heat and flavour.
2. Pour the hot tea over the rice and toppings, so the rice is fully submerged by about 5mm. While some of the toppings can be added or subtracted, *nori* seaweed is a key player, so be sure to add a sprinkle.
3. Make sure that all the flavourings are mixed in well before tucking in.

Note: Leftover rice is perfect for *ocha zuke*; just take care, as it can cause food poisoning if not stored properly and reheated thoroughly. *Ocha zuke* works best with short-grain rice, but you could also attempt it with other varieties, although I think the results will be slightly different.

Wagashi – Traditional Japanese Confectionery

You might have some *wagashi*, or traditional Japanese confectionery, with your tea. They're usually made from plant-based ingredients – *mochi* are like glutinous rice cakes and they can have fillings like *anko* (a sweet red-bean paste made with azuki beans).

Here are my top four favourite *wagashi* to have with tea:

1. ***Daifuku* – rice cake.** A *daifuku* is a small, round *mochi* or glutinous rice cake, stuffed with a delicious filling of some kind. The most traditional filling would be *anko*, but you can also get them with flavoured creams, like strawberry or coffee. They come in pale, pastel colours – usually pink, white or green – and are dusted with a layer of cornflour to prevent them from sticking together.

2. ***Dorayaki* – stuffed castella cake.** Similar to *daifuku*, a *dorayaki* would also typically be stuffed with a red-bean *anko* paste, but the outer layer would be made from castella. Castella is my absolute weakness, and a product of Japan's rich culinary history that I find absolutely fascinating. Nagasaki is now famed for its castella, but the dessert is actually a Portuguese import from the sixteenth century, originally known as *Pao de Castela*. It's made from sugar, flour, eggs and starch syrup. While it has the texture of a light sponge cake, the addition of eggs makes the flavour slightly more complex, a little like a Madeira cake. You can also get matcha varieties, but my favourite is definitely *dorayaki*, in which two discs of castella envelop a little of the sweet mixture.

Japonisme

3. *Taiyaki* – fish cake. This is a deceptive one, as its name is rather
misleading and wouldn't necessarily suggest a sweet dessert.
Taiyaki, or 'baked sea bream', actually features no fish whatsoever.
It is, in fact, a fish-shaped cake, made with a batter similar to
waffles or pancakes, usually filled with a sweet filling. Again, *anko*
is pretty standard, but my favourite is custard – and you can even
get sweet-potato ones. These are best eaten fresh, straight out of
the fish-shaped irons. You usually tend to find them at festivals.
Around New Year, in particular, a lot of food stands will set up near
the temples, and it was around this time of year that I had the best
taiyaki ever, near Gion, in Kyoto. I probably had about three custard
ones, as I couldn't get enough of that deliciously warm sweet pastry
with the beautiful creamy filling.

4. *Yokan* – red-bean jelly. *Yokan* is one of the oldest and more
traditional *wagashi*. It has an extremely subtle flavour and an
unusual texture. It's a jellied dessert made from *azuki* (red bean)
paste, usually bought in blocks and sliced, with several varieties,
some containing nuts, like chestnuts, and fruits, like figs. The jelly-
like texture comes from the beans in combination with the agar and
sugar. *Yokan* is given as a gift, traditionally, and the fact that it is
(mostly) vegan is a nod to ancient Buddhist principles (although
it's always worth double-checking that agar has been used before
being tempted to get some for your vegan friends).

The principles behind tea ceremony – harmony, respect, purity and tranquillity – are what we all aspire to in our lives. As human beings, we want to live peacefully with others and to be respected. By performing the ceremony for others, you provide both them and yourself with a physical manifestation or expression of that desire. It can also help to build a sense of community and solidarity. But we don't have to execute it so formally; having people round for tea can do the same thing in smaller, subtler ways, even if it is just catching up over a brew.

Onsen

温泉とお風呂

Hot springs and bathing

Some of my favourite memories involve going up to my aunt's summer home in Kusatsu, a hot-spring resort, north of Tokyo. The strong smell of sulphur, and the flavour of the famous *manju*, a sweet bun filled with red bean paste, always remind me of my time there. We would go in the winter, to enjoy the *onsen* after a day on the slopes, and in the summer months, too, when the heat of the hot springs would make us feel so refreshed, making the sticky summer air feel a little cooler, and the heat just that little bit more manageable.

Unsurprising for such a volcanic country, *onsens* are dotted all over the place in Japan. There are outdoor and indoor *onsens*, which are different from public bathhouses (*sento*), as they are heated naturally through the springs.

A trip to an *onsen* is very much a communal activity. I usually went with my family, but it's not unusual for people to go with their friends or co-workers. While I can't imagine stripping down to my birthday suit with friends or colleagues over here, it's really common in Japan, and it tends to bring people closer together. I'm not sure whether, for me, this is psychological, inasmuch as it's associated with becoming clean, or because I'm already exposed physically, but some of the most frank, honest and open discussions I've ever had with family members have taken place in an *onsen* environment. Perhaps it has something to do with coming clean in more ways than one?

Onsen Etiquette

Traditionally, both men and women bathed in the same area, but these days that is quite unusual and most *onsens* are split into separate male and female baths.

Whether you're bathing in an indoor or outdoor bath, the rules are the same – you'll be expected to strip off completely. *Onsen* hygiene is taken really seriously. You have to wash off at a bathing station before entering the pool, usually sitting down on a bamboo stool, and using a bamboo bucket to wash your body with soap before entering the communal area. Your hair should be tied up, if it's long, and you need to rinse off all the soap suds before you get in, so you don't cloud the water or cause any interactions with the minerals of the spring.

Tattoo Taboo

A few years ago, my little sister, Amy, came home covered with multiple tattoos, making us groan with frustration as, in the past, many *onsen* operators have banned bathers with tattoos, ostensibly to keep out *yakuza*, or criminal gang members. However, in recent years some have softened in their approach, and you can go in as long as any tattoos are covered with plasters. Just something you might want to consider if you're thinking about getting some ink work done before a big trip!

o   **Putting On a Yukata Kimono – How to Do It**

When you go to a hot-spring resort like Kusatsu, it's really common to
see folks wearing *yukata*. A *yukata* is a casual cotton kimono worn in
the summer. The type you'd find in a *ryokan* (a traditional inn) near an
onsen tends to be dark blue and white, and super comfortable. They
look great, and double up as loungewear, pyjamas or a bathrobe,
without making you look like a lazy slob. The thing I love most about
kimonos is that they flatter every body shape – and there are so
many useful places to stash things, too. A breezy *yukata* combined
with some clunky wooden *geta* (raised-platform) sandals makes the
ultimate summer outfit in an onsen town. Here's how you put one on:

1. Slip your arms into the sleeves
   of your *yukata*. Pretending
   you're a bird and using the
   sleeves to flap like wings is
   entirely optional (but almost
   irresistible).
2. At waist level, grab the hem/
   lapel of the robe in each hand.
3. Pull the right lapel of the robe
   towards the left side of your
   body, just underneath the
   crook of your arm. Make sure
   that the right-hand side of the
   robe isn't on top – it's really
   important because having the

right side of the robe on top
is reserved for the deceased,
when they are dressed for
burial, so doing it that way
round is a massive faux pas.
4. Pull the left side of the robe
   on top, closing the robe at
   the front so that it wraps
   around you. Make sure it's
   snug, so you don't run the
   risk of having it fly open, but
   leave enough room so that it's
   comfortable (or, in my case,
   so that I won't feel restricted
   after stuffing my face with

manju buns). Hold it in place while you get your *obi* belt.

5. If you're female, wrap the *obi* belt around your waist, starting at the front and crossing at the back; for men, it tends to lie lower on the hips. Bring the two ends of the *obi* together and tie it at the front, just off-centre, slightly to the right.

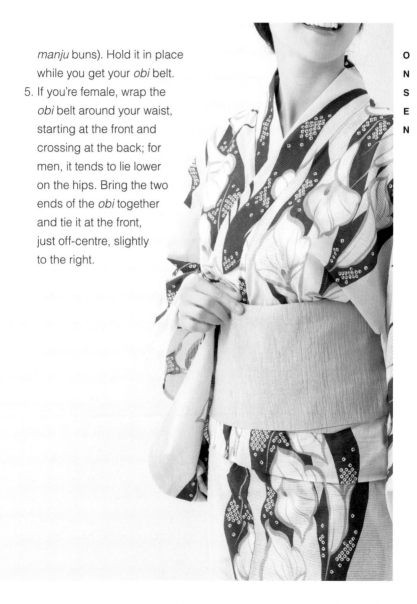

Bathing at Home

It's not just about trips to the *onsen*; baths at home (*furo*) are also a big deal. There is nothing I enjoy more than a good soak at the end of the day, and having navigated the London rental housing market for quite a few years now, there is one non-negotiable requirement: my home must have a bathtub.

My grandfather would take around three baths a day, especially in the summer, when he'd pop back from the office around lunchtime for a quick soak. Japanese baths tend to be extremely deep, meaning that you can get in right up to your shoulders – and most come equipped with a button that lets you reheat the bathwater, so you can easily spend hours in the tub letting your fingertips get all prune-like.

In Japanese homes, the bathroom is usually a wet room, so you would rinse your body off with soap and a shower head, or with some water in a bamboo bucket, before getting in the tub. Getting in the bath isn't about cleaning your body – that all happens outside. Being in the bathtub is about relaxing, letting your body loosen up and releasing tension. It's also the perfect time to reflect, prioritise and let go – letting all your frustrations drain away, along with the water.

Making Your Own Bath Salts

One of the things I stock up on every time I go back to Tokyo is bath salts, as well as bath bombs. There are so many varieties, and the benefits of aromatherapy are great. As we saw in the chapter about *shinrin-yoku* (forest bathing), the phytoncides and chemicals released by the trees have positive health effects – and aromatherapy can have a similarly calming and relaxing influence on the body.

The *onsen* experience is all about scent – whether it's the smell of the sulphur or of hot, clean towels, fresh laundry or soap, it's very much an activity that engages your sense of smell.

Homemade bath salts make excellent gifts.

You will need:

- 700g Epsom salt
- 475g coarse sea salt
- 120g bicarbonate of soda
- essential oils (such as camphor, cypress, rose, orange blossom, eucalyptus, mint, chamomile, lemon balm or lavender)
- fresh herbs, optional (for example, mint, rosemary, lemon balm leaf, jasmine, calendula, ginger)

Combine the Epsom salt, sea salt and bicarbonate of soda in a glass jar. Add a few drops of your chosen essential oil until you get the desired aroma. Really high-quality, pure essential oils tend to be quite pricey, so I'd stick to about 10 drops at most. Adding a few sprigs of herbs always creates a nice effect – particularly mint leaves or some rosemary. The final product will make your bathroom smell utterly divine.

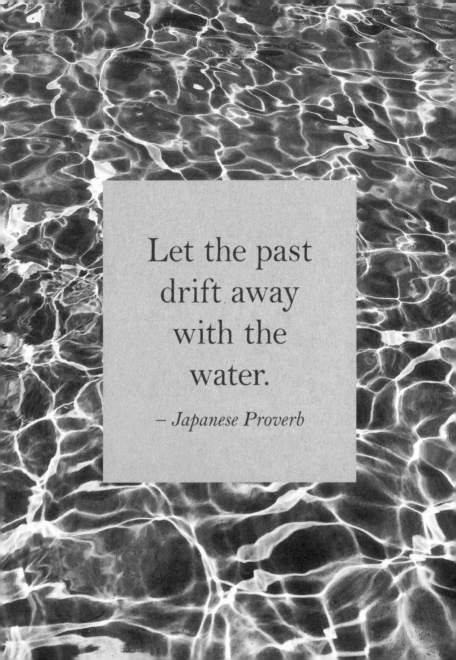

Let the past
drift away
with the
water.

– Japanese Proverb

Getting the Onsen Benefits Abroad

Taking a good, long soak in the tub might seem to be the closest you can get to replicating the experience of going to an *onsen*, but there are other things you can do.

There is something immensely satisfying about the sensation of having water flow over you, and some of the benefits of *onsen* come from simply being in the water – from the water pressure and the buoyancy. My love of *onsen* also might also be at the root of my love for swimming in cold, open bodies of water. My English family can't get enough of outdoor swimming, particularly in rivers in the summertime. Once you get past the first few seconds (which are undoubtedly pretty grim), and get your body moving, it feels amazing – and is sure to get your heart rate up, too.

You could also try going in a sauna; the heat can help increase blood flow and aid in relaxation. The sensation of being immersed in the heat is very similar to an *onsen* and, as such, can help to create a similar frame of mind.

> Bathing is not just about a quick rinse. Taking care of your whole self is essential in maintaining balance and contentment. And rituals around bathing play their part – they provide time in the day when you can focus on yourself, and clear your mind and body. Again, it's an activity that the Japanese take slowly and spend quality time on.

Calligraphy

書道、習字と炭絵

Penmanship and sumi-e

I often joke that I got my expert liquid-eyeliner technique through calligraphy lessons from my grandmother Motoko. While it's true that I do have a deft hand in that department, there are also a few other things I learned from her love of the art.

Born in Russia, during the Second World War, my grandmother wasn't educated in the traditional Japanese way for the first few years of her life. Things like *kakijun* (the order of the strokes when you are writing Japanese characters) was something she learned a little later than some of her peers and, as a result, she is quite self-conscious about her handwriting. But she has practised for years, and has reached a level where she is now qualified to instruct others in the art; so it never ceases to amuse me when she tries to fob the job of writing thank-you cards off on one of my cousins or aunts instead.

I've always found my grandmother's love of *shodo* and *shuji* fascinating – the fact that simply changing the implements for the same set of movements could elicit such a different response from her in terms of how confident she felt in presenting her work to others. In my grandmother's mind, however, they are two different things entirely: *shodo* and *shuji* are an expression of herself at a particular moment in time. Like *sado* (the 'way of tea'), and *kado* (the 'way of flowers'), the word *shodo* refers to the art, or the 'way of calligraphy'. *Shuji*, on the other hand, refers more to penmanship, rather than calligraphy. *Shuji* is taught in schools from an elementary level – so children need to learn the basic strokes and how to hold the brush, before aspiring to become practitioners of the art form.

What is so compelling about *shodo* is the overt role that the calligrapher plays in creating a composition. The paper isn't forgiving – once the ink and brush hit the surface, the calligrapher is committed and has to move with purpose to reach their desired result. Any hesitation or a shaky hand is easily transcribed and captured for ever; the creator is always leaving a part of themselves behind in the piece, adding to its beauty.

In some ways, the different arts are interconnected. For example, before a tea ceremony, you might cast your eye over a work of *shodo* to clear your mind. The piece wouldn't be chosen at random; it would be painstakingly considered, and through it you would get a sense of the atmosphere the host is trying to create by setting the theme, and putting the work on display for the tea ceremony.

Every brushstroke
has a certain tension, a
certain nervousness. Every
brushstroke is, in a sense,
some kind of an accident.

– Raphael Soyer

The Instruments

When I was about eight years old, my grandmother gave me a calligraphy set. I was so enamoured of it that I only opened it occasionally to admire it, before closing it, untouched (and in my mind, unsullied).

The four core tools are referred to as 'treasures of the study', or *bunbo shiho*, and they are as follows:

—The brush: fude
The brush, called the *fude*, has a handle traditionally made from wood or bamboo and bristles made from animal hair of some kind (horse, goat or sheep). Different brushes are used for different strokes: a *futofude*, a thick brush, for big characters and a *hosofude*, or thin brush, for the smaller, more delicate, ones.

—The ink: sumi
The ink (*sumi*) comes in an ink-stick form. In the past, this had a practical purpose, as it was easier to transport long distances. *Sumi* is usually made from a mixture of soot and animal glue, and is often given as a traditional gift, although you can now also get pre-bottled *sumi*.

—The canvas: washi paper

Washi paper is a bit more durable than ordinary paper, and is usually made with mulberry (*kozo*) fibres. *Washi* paper can come in beautiful, textured patterns. *Washi* tape is also great for decorating and general arts and crafts.

—The ink stone: suzuri

The *sumi* ink stick is a block of black pigment that requires dilution. It is ground in the ink stone with some water, as you would do with watercolour paints. Then you dip your brush into the well of the *suzuri* – achieving the right opacity and consistency is part of perfecting the art (but if you're feeling lazy, you can always pour a bit of pre-made bottled ink in there, too).

Besides the four core instruments, you would also use the following when practising the art of calligraphy:

• **A paperweight or *bunchin.*** This keeps everything in its correct place as you work.

• **An under-sheet or *shitajiki.*** You would place a *shitajiki* under the canvas to prevent the ink from bleeding through to whatever is underneath. Traditionally, you might use something like a cloth, but school students in Japan also use plastic ones to prevent their class notes from bleeding through the pages of their notebooks.

• **The seal or *indei.*** A student or practitioner might carve their own seal or stamp (known as an *inkan*), usually with red ink (or *indei*), to mark their work as their own. It would usually be the only burst of colour on an otherwise monochromatic piece.

• ***Fudepen.*** If you were keen to practise your calligraphy without having to fork out for all of the instruments, I'd definitely invest in a *fudepen*. The tip is made with bristles, and it is a portable, easy-to-use way to practise your penmanship and achieve the desired effect without having to get all of your kit ready.

Strokes and Styles

The *eiji happo* are the eight essential strokes in Japanese calligraphy. Every *kanji* character (*kanji* being the Japanese system of writing that utilises Chinese characters) will be made up of one of these, all of which can be found in the character 永 (*ei*, meaning eternal). Practising this character would be a great place for a beginner to start. It's basically the *kanji* equivalent of 'Stairway to Heaven' for people who are learning guitar for the first time.

The *eiji happo* strokes are:

- 側 ***soku***: the dot
- 勒 ***roku***: a horizontal stroke
- 努 ***do***: a vertical stroke
- 趯 ***teki***: an upward flick from a horizontal or vertical stroke (*roku* or *do*)
- 策 ***saku***: an upward flick to the right
- 掠 ***ryaku***: a downward stroke to the left
- 啄 ***taku***: a downward flick to the left
- 磔 ***taku***: a downward stroke to the right.

There are three basic writing styles of *shodo* that have emerged and evolved over time:

1. Kaisho (standardised)

This standardised style is the easiest to read and closest in form to what you might see on a computer, or written down. It isn't highly stylised; it is, however, prescriptive, and requires precision in the way that the stroke order is followed.

2. Gyosho (semi-cursive)

Gyosho relies less on the definition of the strokes, and more on how each character flows into the next one, and the relationship between them.

3. Sosho (abstract)

Sosho is the most abstract of the three basic writing styles, and should evoke a sense of the wind blowing through grass. The focus is less on legibility, and more on conveying an emotion and aesthetic quality.

書家古巷

中國珠海唐家灣

善墨書舍 汪子善書

Sumi-e – Monochromatic Ink-wash Painting

Sumi-e refers to Japanese ink-wash painting, using the *fude* brush and *sumi* ink (see page 230). The focus is on capturing the essence, or the spirit, of the subject without depending on different hues, which can be distracting.

Playing with the white space, and changing the tone of the black ink, can open up so many possibilities. Creativity flourishes within these limitations – and because of this, *sumi-e* really is all about capturing the bigger picture, rather than the smaller, more intricate details. You have to make every stroke meaningful and powerful.

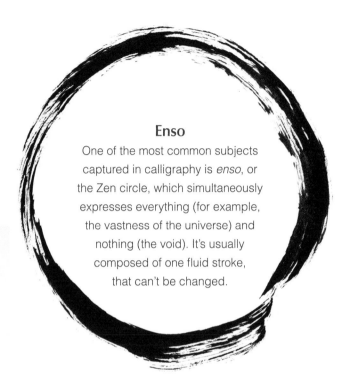

Enso

One of the most common subjects
captured in calligraphy is *enso*, or
the Zen circle, which simultaneously
expresses everything (for example,
the vastness of the universe) and
nothing (the void). It's usually
composed of one fluid stroke,
that can't be changed.

Three Good Reasons Why You Should Practise Calligraphy

- A handwritten or personally inked note will always appear more thoughtful than a text.

- Writing by hand can help to engage and stimulate parts of your brain that deal with memory formation.

- Calligraphy requires concentration and discipline. It's good to be challenged, and not just have the option to hit the return key on your keyboard.

Practice Makes Perfect

The most important thing about getting started with calligraphy is learning your angles. Where should you hold the brush to get a thicker or thinner stroke? Do you start heavy-handed, before going lighter? How much pressure do you apply to achieve the desired flicks?

These are not the kind of things that anyone else can teach you. You have to learn your own limits and get to know the way your body interacts with and controls the brush. Use scrap paper to practise, practise, practise, figuring out how to let the characters flow before committing it all to canvas.

As a digital consultant, I found myself with a wealth of beautiful stationery and pens, but couldn't remember the last time I'd handwritten anything. So a year ago, I began keeping a written journal. There is something a bit more formal about writing something out by hand; it leaves more of an impression, requires so much more thought and is more of a considered activity – one that isn't so conducive to recklessness. And receiving a handwritten note always feels much more meaningful. Even if you're not skilled in penmanship, seeing and reading your own handwriting can bring to the fore aspects of yourself you might not have thought about in a while.

Since writing my journal I have also found that I am remembering things a bit more. It turns out this isn't just anecdotal – there are studies that have shown the benefits of hand writing, especially when it comes to retaining new information. One study[5] showed that the brains of children who had to write out words by hand 'lit up' more than their peers. It's also nice to get away from the screen once in a while.

So next time, don't type it, pick up a pen and write it down instead. Try it. It might just surprise you.

The
Japanese
home

T H E   J A P A N E S E   H O M E

Although my grandparents spent most of their time in the house in Tokyo, my grandfather always said he felt more at home in the Kamakura house. He loved and cherished that place. Unlike his Tokyo apartment, it was architecturally more traditionally Japanese, with an exterior hallway outside the house, sliding paper doors, a garden with a tiny orange tree and a stone *tōrō* lantern.

The smell of *tatami* floors, which to me is not dissimilar to caramel, always reminds me of my holidays spent there. The sliding doors, the deep baths and the reliance on space heaters in the winter make me grateful for having been able
to spend so many visits in what to me is a traditional Japanese home.

It wasn't just in Japan that I grew up in a Japanese home. My grandfather influenced my mother in many ways (a fierce stubbornness, for one thing), and you could trace his influence to the home I grew up in with her in New York. They both hated clutter, periodically having massive clear-outs when the feeling took them; they shared a love of plants and both loved being in the kitchen, being the most passionate and talented cooks in the family.

Noren, traditional Japanese fabric dividers, would hang in the doorways of our house and there was always a spare set of futon tucked in the wardrobe when friends needed to stay (usually if she had hosted a dinner party, and they were too stuffed to leave).

My mother tends to move around quite a bit, but wherever she is, it always feels like her home – familiar, comforting and very much representative of her background and identity.

Inside and Outside: Separation of Space in the Japanese Home

One of my earliest memories of my return to the UK, after living for several years in Japan as a child, was of me dutifully packing my *uwabaki,* or 'indoor shoes', into my book bag for my first day of school. No other memory so acutely highlights for me the separation between indoor and outdoor space in Japanese culture. It's so ingrained that the movements and ritual when entering a space come naturally. When visiting a shrine, you'd bow respectfully before entering, and you'd perform *temizu* – pouring clean water over your left hand, then your right, before swishing water in your mouth to purify yourself. You'd also remove your shoes before entering a building, as a matter of course.

The rigid separation between indoor and outdoor space also extends to the home. *Te-arai* (washing) and *ugai* (gargling and rinsing out your mouth or throat) are common practice when you come home, whether you're a school child or an overworked businessman. As you enter, you want to cleanse yourself of impurities (bacteria, for example), or even just change your frame of mind.

Home is
where you
make it.

– Japanese proverb

Japonisme

Home Comforts: Traditional Staples in Japanese Dwellings

A few years ago, my Japanese grandmother came to stay with me for a couple of weeks in a tiny flat I lived in with my partner at the time. I would spend most of the day at work, leaving her in the care of my sister, and catch up in the evenings. On the second night of her visit, my sister remarked in amusement on the transformation of my entryway. My shoes had all been spirited away from my wardrobe and placed by the front door, and I'd suddenly become the owner of several pairs of slippers to provide to future houseguests. The lack of a traditional entryway or separation was clearly unsettling for my grandmother, and she chose to tell me in a subtle, understated sort of way.

Homes and styles have, of course, changed over time, but there are elements that have become cultural mainstays, making up an authentically Japanese home.

Genkan

Usually, every home in Japan has a *genkan*, or a traditional entryway. It's a symbolic border – generally raised – between the internal and the external, although a lot of homes today are being built without one. For a place whose primary purpose serves as the location for the removal of footwear, it is charged with meaning and etiquette around it is strictly observed: upon entry, shoes are removed, and turned inward to face the door or put in *getabako*, 'a clog box'. Of course, in practical terms, the *genkan* ritual provides the added benefit of having to vacuum a whole lot less, and being far more hygienic, too.

You always show your own *genkan* respect, but this is heightened when entering someone else's home. As you enter, you offer the standard greeting of *ojamashimasu*, the closest translation of which would be 'I'm going to disturb you', or, 'I'm going to be in your way'. The connotations are (usually) far from negative; rather, they are an acknowledgement of the imposition on the host, and a reference to the hospitality you're about to receive. It's a little apologetic, and more deferential, in that you are recognising that you are going to be in your host's personal space, potentially in their way, and dependent on them within it. This greeting is telling of the wider cultural respect for the space of others, and of communal space as well. It can be seen in the cleanliness of public spaces, like the streets, subways and parks in Japan.

Entering a shared space reveals so much about Japanese culture, philosophies and ideals. There's a lot to be learned; the ritualistic separation and respect that come from this way of life make me an excellent house guest (if only at first).

Wooden Accents

There tend to be a lot of wood accents in Japanese homes, which really tie into the whole *wabi-sabi* aesthetic – the changes in patinas being seen as beautiful. So you wouldn't paint over them – rather, you would appreciate the beauty in the way that the wood changes over time.

And it's not just about wood, but many organic materials. How can you incorporate them into your home? How will they wither, age and change character over time? How you can help to preserve and maintain these pieces to ensure they are structurally sound and restore any cracks that may damage their foundations, while allowing them to age naturally. They should be aged or withered beautifully, not scruffy or unkempt.

Tokonoma (Alcoves)

Tokonoma are built-in alcove-like spaces where art like *shodo*, or even living art, such as *ikebana* or *bonsai*, can be displayed. The architect Frank Lloyd Wright compared the Japanese *tokonoma* to its Western counterpart – the fireplace.

Kotatsu (Heated tables and blankets)

Japanese homes don't tend to be heated centrally, and rely on space heaters instead. A *kotatsu* comprises a low table with a duvet attached and a heater underneath, making it possibly the cosiest place on earth. There is something really satisfying about leaving the warmth of the *kotatsu* to go and make a cup of tea, and then getting settled back in. If I'm in Japan in the winter, you will most likely find me in one. I've even been known to leave my bed and very happily sleep there. The closest I can get to it over here is probably just a duvet and a hot-water bottle, which does the trick (especially in winter).

At the Table – Chabudai and Zabuton

For me, the most important piece of furniture is the dining table – it's where people gather and congregate, the heart of the home.

It's pretty common and traditional for the main table of the house to be a *chabudai*. A *chabudai* is a low table, perhaps half a metre off the floor at most, that can easily be folded and stored away for convenience. As it is so low, you sit on your knees on a *zabuton*, a thin type of floor cushion. Sitting in this way is really great for your posture, particularly for your back. I'm so used to sitting like this that I usually eat my dinner at home this way, at my coffee table, rather than sitting up in a chair!

Transformative Spaces

The key takeaway about Japanese homes for me is the fact that they are so changeable. This is something I still struggle with because I like my personal living space, and my own room especially, to look a particular way. I can always tell when someone has been in my room while I've been out, if my pillows are in disarray, for example, or my chair has been moved slightly. Living like this isn't realistic though, because very few people live in such rigid isolation. Friends come to stay, younger siblings get marker pen on different surfaces and there are always the inevitable red-wine stains on the new white carpet.

Perhaps because Japan is so prone to earthquakes, tsunamis and other natural disasters, its homes and architecture are planned to be a bit more dynamic and fluid. Design focuses around withering, rusting and ageing, and things are intended to be moved around and shifted. It's also an incredibly small island that is extremely densely populated, so space is precious, and there simply isn't room for clutter. Rigidly defined rooms with set purposes are not, therefore, practical and, in many ways, the fluidity makes these spaces a lot more liveable.

While I'm not advocating knocking down the walls of your home, taking a different approach to the way you look at space and what you use your rooms for might be a refreshing and clarifying exercise. It will also help you to re-evaluate your possessions and 'stuff' (see page 256). Fluidity and flexibility should, I believe, always be welcomed, although, as I said, this is something I sometimes struggle with personally.

Making Use of Space and Multi-functional Rooms

Most Japanese houses won't have designated or set uses for particular rooms, other than the *genkan*, kitchen and bathroom. Rooms are partitioned off by moveable *fusuma* (sliding doors) or *shoji* (translucent paper and wood room dividers), which run along wooden rails, saving on space and making the rooms within a home a lot more flowing and adaptable than they might otherwise be.

The living area (or *ima*) is usually at the centre of the house and the surrounding partitions might be removable to make more space, if needed.

And even when the rest of the house is built in a Western style, most Japanese homes will have a *washitsu* – a Japanese-style room with *tatami* (woven rice straw mat) flooring.

—Futon

Futons in Japan aren't synonyms for sofa beds, as they are in the West. When a Japanese person refers to a futon, they're talking about a mattress set that includes a foldable mattress (*shikibuton*) and a duvet (*kakebuton*) that can be stored neatly away. This means a room can be used for other activities besides sleep, like hanging laundry or exercise.

De-cluttering, Storage and Organisation

T
H
E

J
A
P
A
N
E
S
E

H
O
M
E

The key to conserving space is organisation and keeping things as streamlined as possible. A lot of it has to do with useful storage solutions (I aspire to make my house look like the inside of a Muji store), but it's also about getting rid of all of the clutter that accumulates over time. Do you really need it? When was the last time you used it? Does it make you happy?

When I was younger, I used to get incredibly sentimental about objects and possessions, but since moving abroad, living in shared houses and darting around the London rental market, I think I've got it down.

Here are a few of my top de-cluttering tips:

• The clothes-hanger trick

Spend some time sorting through your clothes, and hang them with the hooks of the hangers facing outwards (towards you). When you return clothes to the wardrobe after wearing them, you will automatically hang them the other way. After six months, take a look at the items on hangers that are still in the same position they were six months before (that ill-fitting dress you got on sale, or the blouse with the ink stain on it) – they can probably go to the charity shop. I do this regularly, and it makes me way more disciplined about buying clothes that, to be honest, I really don't need.

- **Clothes swap**

  After I do the clothes-hanger trick, I like to invite a few friends over, and get them to bring along some of their unloved items. Then we do a swap. This has all the benefits of shopping, but without making a dent in your wallet. And it's really nice to see some previously neglected items put to good use, too.

- **One step at a time**

  A few times a month, I will spend an evening or a weekend afternoon tackling one part of a room – whether it's that drawer full or chargers for phones I don't own any more, out-of-season clothing or that dodgy neon and glitter-covered music festival gear. Taking it one step at a time makes it a whole lot more manageable.

Speaking of Clutter – Do You Tsundoku?

I've become fairly disciplined about de-cluttering when it comes to objects like clothes. I've resigned myself to the fact that I don't really care enough about fashion to spend time, money and resources on it. I am, however, totally guilty of another type of clutter.

There is a word in Japanese – *tsundoku* – which describes the phenomenon of accumulating books that remain unread. There are so many books I've bought, and have been meaning to read, but the time in which to do so has eluded me. My task, next new year, is to tackle the pile of books that I've collected (or '*tsundoku*'-ed) . . .

Top Three Tips for Creating a Japanese-inspired Home

When I was growing up, my mother was really house-proud, and we lived in a beautiful flat in an old and dilapidated townhouse near Central Park in New York. It was a tiny apartment, but it never felt that way thanks to her love of traditional Japanese aesthetics, features like screens and plants and having only a few pieces of furniture. Inspired by her, here are three tips for making a house feel like a home, the Japanese way:

1. Bring the outdoors in

Whether it's with plants or wooden accents, try bringing the natural world indoors. The Japanese design aesthetic is heavily influenced by the interplay between society and humanity and their relationship with the natural world. We always had several plants at home, particularly by the window. And rather than making the room seem darker, they made it seem bigger, somehow.

2. Keep it minimal

Clear your environment of clutter – it'll make things easier to find and clean, and look a lot sleeker, too. Sort through your wardrobes, be more strategic with space and make do with what you have; buying new things and furniture should be a last resort. Think about ways in which you can recycle and upcycle thoughtfully, too. Less is definitely more.

3. Experiment with space

A few clever storage hacks and you can find multiple uses for the same room or space. A guest room can also double up as a meditation room, for example. In my home, by investing in a good laundry rack, we changed an awkward alcove from a storage dump to a display area for beautiful plants – we've currently got some beautiful pussy willow and eucalyptus there, and it makes for an infinitely nicer living environment. You can go to Japanese furniture stores for inspiration, or check them out online. Finding clever storage solutions means you can avoid the curse of the scary drawer/wardrobe (you know, the one where you stash random things so you don't have to deal with them . . .).

Investing time and energy in making your home a beautiful, happy space is always worthwhile. A clean and organised home can help you to see things more clearly – rushing around trying to find things when you're in a panic can be so stressful. So eliminating that source of stress can make an enormous difference to both your sanity and overall wellbeing.

We are naturally territorial creatures, and need our own havens to retreat back to, so respect your own space, and also that of others – you will thank yourself.

03

Shukanka

習慣化

Forming the habit

S The monotony of *kakijun* – the order of strokes when writing
H characters – was the bane of my Japanese Saturday-school
U existence as a child. I found it profoundly unfair that my classmates
K and school friends got to spend their Saturdays together in the Girl
A Scouts, presumably toasting marshmallows, going sailing and tying
N knots, while I sat writing the same character over and over and over
K again, in the exact same order, for what felt like days.
A   Repetition, willpower and self-discipline are things that need to
be taught; they really don't come naturally to most. Once you form
the habit, though, it sticks, and that's where the real benefit comes
in. Whether it's finding the discipline to exercise, live in a clean,
organised home or make the time to accomplish all the tasks you
want to get done – putting in the legwork from the beginning makes
it so much simpler further down the line.

It's all about a larger journey: your work is never done, and the
habit is something (annoyingly) you won't be able to tick off of your
to-do list. You should always be iterating: constantly improving,
shifting your method and challenging yourself. *Kaizen, shukanka*
– these are all things that are taken for granted. But they have the
power to transform your life, and simplify aspects of it in the process.

It's not about getting things perfect, or setting unrealistic standards
for yourself. There is a saying, *Naseba naru*, which roughly translates
as, 'If you take action, it will happen'. It's about the bigger picture. You
tend to regret the things you don't do over the things you've done. And
isn't that what living a happy and fulfilled life is all about?

At the same time, things don't happen overnight. They take time,
cultivation and dedication, as well as sweat and, possibly, some
tears in the process.

Beginning
is easy.
Continuing
is hard.

– Japanese proverb

S H U K A N K A Left to my own devices, I have the potential to be incredibly lazy. I could sleep in for hours, eat junk food for days and binge watch episodes of endless series on Netflix. I've done it before, many years ago, and it was probably during the unhappiest period of my life. Now, I'm constantly rushed off my feet, but I've started to get the right balance: I give my personal life and health equal priority, and find time to create things that make me happy. Achieving this balance has taken a good while, and it's nowhere near perfect yet, either. But I'm definitely on the right track.

The idea is to think long-term about how you can take the philosophies and practices in this book and incorporate them into your life. It's all about habit forming – and once you crack that, you begin to do it without even thinking about it. In this section, we look at the strategies and ways in which real, tangible and long-term change happens.

And as for those Japanese classes on Saturday that seemed like such a chore growing up . . . they've actually shaped me so much as a person: I'm fairly efficient when it comes to my free time as a result. And knowing the order of the strokes really does make things easier!

Putting It into Practice

What really struck me when writing this book was how it brought so many things about myself and my family to light.

Conversations with my Aunt Taeko, about tea in particular, really made me think about her constant pursuit of self-improvement and discipline for her art. Having practised tea ceremony for a long time, she has earned the privilege of a *chamei*, or tea name – something that is bestowed on advanced practitioners of tea ceremony. Yet in our discussions, my aunt was really passionate about conveying to me the magnitude of the journey still ahead of her: 'When you are allowed to practise, you don't attain a level, but get permission to learn the next road. There is no end,' she said.

Initially, I found this unsatisfactory. But on further reflection, it seemed so pure, genuine and true. Because are we ever really finished with anything? Things can always be extended, expanded, worked upon further. Let's look at the ways in which we can manage this in our daily lives:

1. The first is by accepting the fact that obstacles – call it failure, stumbling blocks, challenges, what have you – will always arise. They're inevitable but, in the long run, they will serve to make us stronger. One of my favourite sayings in terms of the imagery this evokes is *ame futte ji katamaru*, meaning that 'After the rain, the earth hardens'. Adversity builds character. It also makes us stronger, and our stories a bit more compelling.

2. The second is by taking it incrementally – small steps at a time. Don't get overwhelmed by the bigger picture, or put too much pressure on yourself by taking on too much. Work away diligently, constantly and consistently.

3. The third is by accepting that nothing is ever truly complete. If you stare at anything for long enough, you will always find things to tweak and improve. So it's about finding acceptance and thinking iteratively, rather than in stasis or in isolation. It's something that I still find myself working on, and something I'll always grapple with, I'm sure. But letting go of the things you can't control is crucial.

Kaizen – Changing for the Better

The word '*kaizen*' directly translates as 'improvement', but some might be more familiar with its application in a factory setting. Toyota famously utilised the concept after the Second World War to enhance production and increase efficiency by implementing small, continuous improvement in their manufacturing processes. The ultimate goal for businesses in employing the *kaizen* approach is to eliminate waste and encourage experimentation and self-reflection in an aligned and standardised way.

Applying Kaizen Business Principles to Your Life

While *kaizen*, as a concept, has strong business connotations, its relevance extends far beyond that world.

You're not a well-oiled machine, so applying these apparently mechanical theories to your life might seem incredibly bizarre, but they can provide food for thought. In the past, I've been guilty of repeating the same mistakes, getting myself into what seems to be the same situation over and over again. But having open discussions and harnessing some of these business principles has come in very handy.

—Teamwork

No man is an island, and all that . . .

I still find it hard to ask for help, but whenever I do, I always wonder why it took me so long. Teamwork, building your relationships, both personal and professional – all of this is key. Be a team player. And remember, it's a deal of give and take, too. So if you're free, offer your help; the situation might be reversed further down the line.

Even
monkeys
fall from
trees.

– *Japanese proverb*

—Discipline

Whether it's mustering up the energy to get yourself out of bed to make it to that 6 a.m. yoga class, pre-making your lunches for the week or getting your work done ahead of a deadline, it all takes one thing: discipline. Find that thing that gets you going, whatever it is, and do it. I find it extremely difficult to summon up the motivation to do most things – like doing exercise or completing trivial tasks – without gamifying it somehow, either through list-making apps or justifying certain purchases once I've reached certain goals. I know I should be doing them anyway, but it works for me, and I stand by it!

—Feedback and reflection

Reassessing failures, whether personal or professional, might seem a tad morbid, but it's essential for your peace of mind. Why did you act that way? What would you do next time? Reflecting on yourself, being open in your discussions with others and honest with yourself about your shortcomings can really prevent heartache in the future.

I have a fairly vivid and active imagination, and can often get carried away, or be overly sensitive. Addressing issues and being open can really help counter this and put perceived conflicts or slights into perspective.

There's a great saying about this in Japanese: *Anzuru yori umu ga yasashii* – 'Giving birth to a baby is easier than worrying about it'. It seems to make a lot of sense, but not having been on that journey yet, I'll let the mothers out there get back to me on this . . .

—Maintaining and adhering to standards

Set high standards for yourself, while remaining realistic (and kind). I wholeheartedly believe that comparison is the thief of joy, and that the only person you should be competing against is yourself. Set yourself challenges, and try and beat your personal best. Achieving goals and personal targets can be so rewarding.

—Commitment, authenticity and transparency

Don't be wishy-washy with your goals – commit! Wear your heart on your sleeve. I toyed with the idea of starting with a blog for months, and it was only when I began to tell people about what I was thinking of doing that I actually did anything about it. Once I had put it out there, I had to follow through. So put yourself out there, wear your team colours, pledge your loyalty – and stick to it!

Shukanka: Ways to Make It Stick

Long-term change never happens overnight. It's achieved through softer, subtler techniques. Think baby steps first, before signing up to the marathon. As with *kakijun* strokes, you have to sit there and learn the characters before you can begin writing your epic novel.

Make Lists

Our brains love lists. It's how we make sense of the world, because we process information spatially.

I have lists for everything. If anyone caught sight of the app on my phone, or my book of lists, they would get to know me fairly intimately. While I love writing lists by hand (and I have a verging-on-the-unhealthy supply of the most beautiful stationery to prove it), more recently I've become a fan of digital lists, too. Breaking up tasks into easily digestible chunks makes me feel a whole lot more productive, and keeps me engaged and stimulated without being distracted.

There's even a word in Japanese to describe the feeling of elation you get from finishing a task, whether it's something as mundane as filing your taxes or running across the finish line: *yatta*!

Diarise

I'm a big forward planner, and every Sunday night I fill up a pinboard with my plans for the week ahead – not just dinner reservations or work meetings, either. I also find it really helpful to put reminders in for myself to check in on my mood, re-evaluate personal relationships or conflicts or just trivial events that might have sentimental value.

A Minute a Day

My cousin was on a mission a few years ago to get fitter. After we'd been chatting about it for a while, I was perplexed when a single push-up was all that was eventually achieved. But for them, rather than going full throttle with a new regime, small incremental changes were the key to eventually making it part of a habit: doing one more push-up each day than the day before was the key to making it sustainable for their lifestyle.

What I've Learned

My grandfather passed away suddenly and unexpectedly in December 2011. As a university student at the time, I was able to take advantage of my long winter break and go back to Japan to help take care of my grandmother and provide support as best as I could.

Many Japanese households will have a deep clean (*osouji*) to welcome in the New Year, and start anew. Faced with our recent loss, my grandmother and I stuck to our usual routine. While clearing my grandfather's desk, we came across a white paper box with my name written on it, and emblazoned with the characters of Kasuga Taisha – a grand Shinto shrine in the city of Nara.

Kasuga Taisha is known for the stone lanterns that lead up to it, and through a park full of deer – believed to be sacred messengers. So it was fitting, really, that inside the box was a delicately hand-carved and painted deer, which held a tiny paper scroll in its mouth: my grandfather's final message to me, his first granddaughter.

The scroll contained an *omikuji*, a fortune written on a piece of paper, chosen at random at a temple. If a prediction is bad, the offending *omikuji* is abandoned in the temple grounds, usually tied near a pine tree, or on metal wires set up for the purpose. But my grandfather's final gift to me was *dai-kichi* – a great blessing, and the one that most hope for.

I'm not the most superstitious person, but I find more comfort in the words on that little paper scroll than I'd care to admit. I'd like to think that most of it will come true, in one way or another, but some of the learnings, I think, can be applied more widely.

My Dai-kichi

Lost objects will be found soon; look to find it between other objects.

We often are so focused on meeting a specific target or goal that we forget to take in and be thankful for the things that already surround us, that are already within our grasp and that bring us happiness. Remember to be grateful, appreciate the smaller moments and take in the present, grounding yourself.

The journey; prospects are good, but look out for your companions.

Look beyond yourself, and cherish what is around you: your home, your environment and your work. How can you better yourself by bettering your surroundings? This reminds me of another proverb: 'An apprentice near a temple will recite the scriptures untaught.' We are shaped by our environment, just as we shape it ourselves.

Rely on the advice of others.

Listen to stories, seek new perspectives and change your perceptions.

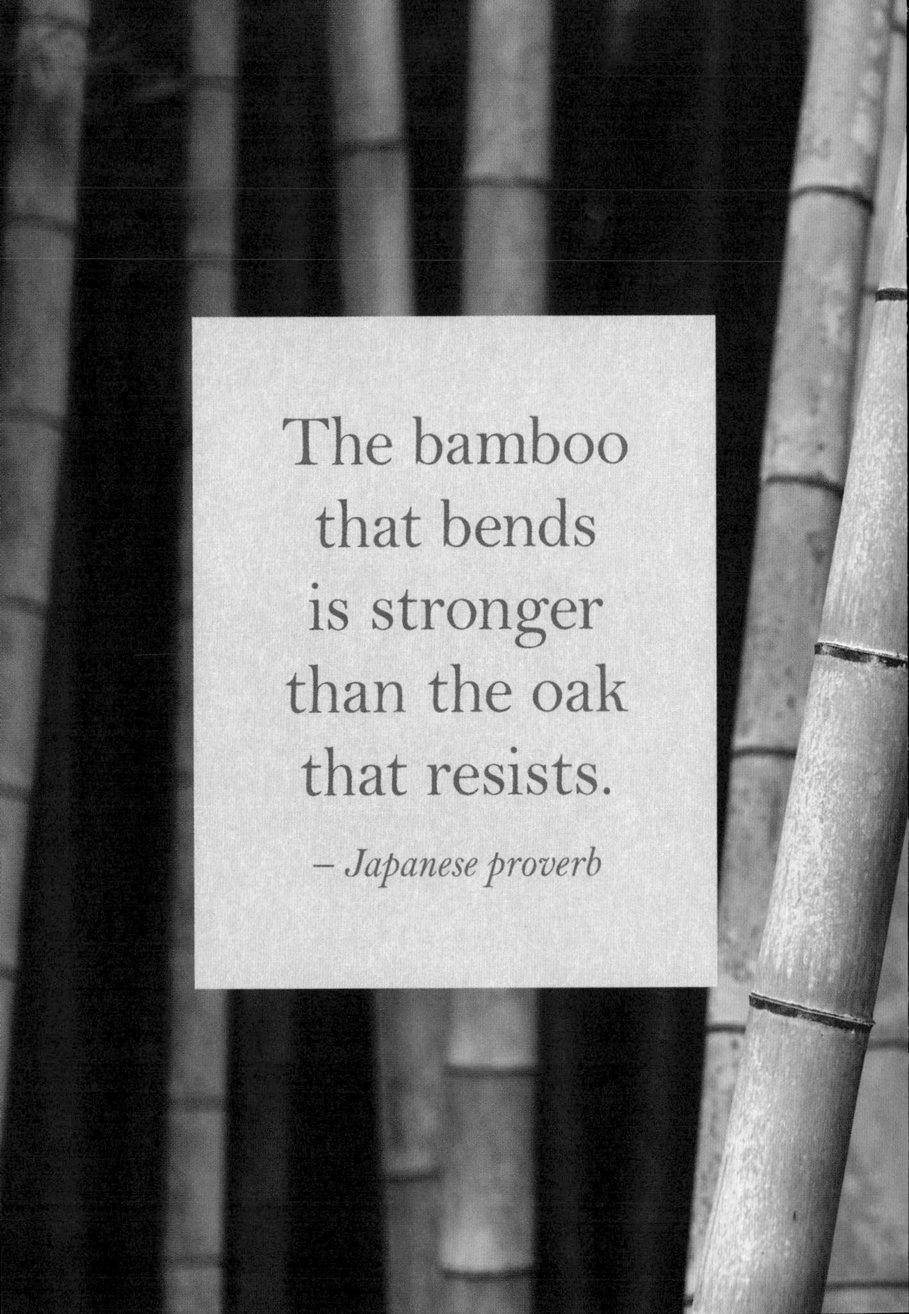

The bamboo
that bends
is stronger
than the oak
that resists.

– Japanese proverb

All of the philosophies, concepts and activities in this book can help you to find contentment and happiness. Your *ikigai* will be your core motivator – your purpose, your reason and your 'why'. Along the way, you'll encounter failure, loss and pain. But instead of despair, they will provide clarity, making things even more beautiful as a result; the broken edges, fixed with gold, will be what make things all the more beautiful. By embracing imperfection and celebrating the seemingly mundane, you'll find value and appreciation in what already lies in front of you.

Changing your mindset doesn't happen overnight. We rarely experience that lightning-bolt moment, and we cannot change our nature so rapidly. But it can come through what we do, and how we do it; by knowing what it is we want to achieve, we can begin to try to get ourselves there. This is achieved through mindfulness – it comes from being present, and listening to ourselves and taking the time for self-care, whether it's through a walk in the woods, arranging flowers, having a good old soak in the bath or organising our homes. It also comes from our relationships with others and with the outside world – through eating with each other, having a cup of tea together or writing a letter to let them know that they are in your thoughts.

Don't rush out and do all of these things at once. It's too much, and far too overwhelming. Rather, be thoughtful and find small and subtle ways to bring these concepts into your routine organically.

Take small, iterative steps. Take the time to check in with yourself and others, and reflect, without being too self-critical.

Find balance, take breaks, savour the silence. Get started.
Embrace the scrapes, scars and grazes you'll get from trying.

Fall down seven times, stand up eight. And keep going.

This is what I want to convey through Japonisme.

A B O U T

T H E

A U T H O R

Erin Niimi Longhurst is a half-Japanese, half-British writer and blogger. She currently works as a social media and digital consultant, helping charities, non-profits and foundations to improve their interactions with those who are important to them, by telling their stories more effectively online. Her blog, Island Bell, focuses on food, travel and lifestyle. She is a graduate of the University of Manchester with a degree in Social Anthropology.

Acknowledgements

So many people made this possible, and there is no way I can thank anyone enough for all of the encouragement and support I've had.

My amazing family, who have had to put up with multiple phone calls at the most awkward hours. My mother, Eriko, my aunts, Taeko and Junko, my grandmother, Motoko and my little sister, Amy.

I'd also like to take this opportunity to publicly acknowledge and thank you for making me go to Japanese school instead of the Girl Scouts like I wanted to, Mama. You were, of course, proven totally right.

Dad and Katie, Rosie and Clement, thank you.

My wonderfully supportive friends and colleagues – you are all incredible. I'm so lucky.

Finally, to everyone at HarperCollins who made this possible, especially Carolyn Thorne, Georgina Atsiaris, Lucy Sykes-Thompson, James Empringham, Jasmine Gordon and Rosie Margesson.

Index

Glossary

Agedashi tofu Deep-fried soybean curd

Ai All-encompassing love

Ame futte ji katamaru The earth hardens after the rain

Anime Hand-drawn or computer animation

Anko Red-bean paste

Anzuru yori umu ga yasashii Giving birth to a baby is easier than worrying about it

Azuki Red bean paste

Bento box A Japanese lunchbox

Bon Festival A Buddhist festival honouring the spirit of one's ancestors

Bonsai Miniature Japanese trees

Bubu arare Rice crackers

Bunbo shiho The treasures of the study, or essential instruments in calligraphy

Bunchin Paperweight

Butsudan A shrine for a deceased relative

Chabana A flower arrangement displayed at tea ceremonies

Chabudai A low table

Chadogu Equipment required for tea ceremony

Cha-ire Tea caddy

Cha-iro Brown, or 'the colour of tea'

Chaji Full-length formal tea ceremony

Chakai Tea ceremony, slightly informal

Chakin White cloth

Chamei Tea name, bestowed upon those attaining a high level in tea ceremony

Chasaku Tea scoop

Chasen Bamboo whisk

Chashitsu Tearoom

Chawan Tea cup or bowl

Chirashi Scattered sushi

Daibutsu Giant Buddha

Daifuku Rice cake

Dai-kichi A great blessing

Dashi Stock

Do (in calligraphy) The vertical stroke

Dorayaki Stuffed castella cake

Eiji happo The eight essential strokes in calligraphy

Enso Zen circle

Fude Calligraphy brush

Fudepen Calligraphy brush pen

Fureai The mutual connection or bond that is formed between generations, or across different professions or vocations within society

Fureai kippu A 'caring relationship' ticket, that can be earned and traded as a form of social currency

Furo Bath

Fusuma Sliding doors

Futon Foldable bedding

Ganbare A motivational chant or saying, meaning do your best, or don't give up

Genen shoyu Low-salt soy sauce

Genkan Entryway

Genmaicha Roasted rice tea

Geta Raised-platform sandals

Getabako Clog or shoe box

Giri-choco Chocolate given out of a sense of social obligation

Gyosho Semi-cursive style of calligraphy

Ha-to A love heart

Haiku A style of poem

Hana yori dango Dumplings over flowers

Hanakotoba The language of flowers

Hara hachi bu Eat until you are 80 per cent full

Hibi A method of repairing through kintsugi, mending a crack

Hikawa maru A great Shinto shrine in Saitama; also the name of an ocean liner travelling between Japan and the United States

Hojicha Roasted green tea

Ikebana The art of flower arranging

Ikigai Purpose for living, or raison d'être

Ima Living area

Indei A seal or stamp

Irusu Pretending to be away when you are really at home

Itadakimasu 'I humbly receive', said before eating a meal, like bon appetit

Iwanu ga hana Not speaking is the flower

Jaku Tranquillity

Jiji Shortened, affectionate name for grandfather (oji-san)

Jiyuka Freestyle *ikebana*

Jushi Additional flowers and plants that make up an *ikebana* arrangement

Kachou fuugetsu The characters for flower, bird, wind and moon, but together they mean learning about yourself through experiencing the beauty of nature

Kadomatsu Traditional New Year decorations

Kaiseki A formal, multi-course meal

Kaishi paper Paper used in tea ceremonies

Kaisho Standardised style of calligraphy

Kaizen Continous improvement

Kake no kintsugi rei Replacing a piece with gold

Kakebuton Duvet

Kakijun The order of strokes when writing Japanese characters

Kanji Japanese character of Chinese origin

Karaage Fried chicken

Karada The body

Karaoke Activity that involves singing along to pre-recorded music – a clipped compound meaning 'empty orchestra' in Japanese

Karoshi Death from overwork

Katsuobushi Bonito flakes

Kawaakari The moonlight reflecting off a river

Kei Respect

Kenzan A flower frog, or a metal spiked disc onto which flowers are stuck

Kiku Chrysanthemum

Kimono Japanese traditional robe

Kintsugi Connecting or repairing with gold

Kogarashi Wind that nudges the leaves off trees

Koi Romantic love

Koicha Thick tea

Koikuchi Dark soy sauce

Kokuhaku A declaration of love

Kokoro The heart and the mind

Komorebi Sunlight that filters through the trees

Konbini Convenience store

Kotatsu A low table with heating

Koukan nikki
A friendship diary that is swapped in rotation among friends

Kozo Mulberry

Kuidaore Going broke from your love of food

Kuishimbo A glutton or a gourmand

Kukicha Twig tea

Maki Roll

Manju Sweet bun filled with red bean paste

Marudaizu shoyu Whole bean soy sauce

Matcha Powdered green tea

Mirin Rice wine used for cooking

Miso Fermented soybean paste

Mochi Glutinous rice cake

Mono no aware The bittersweet nature of being

Moribana An *ikebana* style meaning 'piled-up flowers'

Mugicha Barley tea

Nageire An *ikebana* style meaning 'thrown in'

Naseba naru If you take action, it will happen

Nasu dengaku Miso aubergine

Natsukashii A happy feeling induced by nostalgia

Natto Fermented soybeans

Nigiri Hand-pressed sushi

Nodate Tea ceremony performed al fresco

Nokorimono ni fuku ga aru Luck exists in the leftovers

Noren Japanese fabric dividers for doorways and entrances.

Nori Roasted seaweed

Nippon Japan in Japanese

Obi Belt for a kimono

Ocha Tea

Ocha zuke Tea-topped rice

Oishii Delicious

Ojamashimasu A greeting when entering another's home, meaning 'I am going to get in your way'

Otemae The act of performing tea ceremony

Otsukaresama
A saying that acknowledges the hard work of another

Omikuji A fortune

Onigiri Rice balls

Onsen Hot spring

Osouji Cleaning

Radio taiso Radio calisthenics

Ramen Noodle soup

Rikka Formal, upright style of *ikebana*

Roku (in calligraphy) The horizontal stroke

Ryaku (in calligraphy) The downward stroke to the left

Sado (or chado) The traditional art of tea ceremony

Sakoku Isolationist foreign policy, meaning Japan was a 'closed country' for 220 years to foreign influence

Saku (in calligraphy) Upward flick to the right

Sashimi Raw fish after it has been cleaned and prepared for consumption

Sei Purity

Seika (also known as Shoka) An *ikebana* style that is asymmetric

Seiza Kneeling

Sencha Japanese tea

Sento Public bathhouse

Shibui Muted or understated

Shikibuton Foldable mattress

Shin The longest stem in an *ikebana* arrangement

Shinrin-yoku Forest bathing

Shinzou The heart, when referring to the organ

Shiro shoyu White soy sauce

Shitajiki An under-sheet placed under calligraphy to prevent ink from bleeding through

Shodo The way of calligraphy

Shoganai It cannot be helped

Shoji Paper and wood room dividers

Shoyu Soy sauce

Shuji Penmanship

Shukanka Habit forming

Soe The second-longest stem in an *ikebana* arrangement

Soku (in calligraphy) The dot stroke

Sosho Abstract style of calligraphy

Sudoku A logic-based number game

Sumi Ink

Sumi-e Ink-wash painting

Sushi A Japanese fish and rice dish

Sushi no ko Powdered sushi rice seasoning

Suzuri Inkstone

Tabemono Food

Tai (also known as Hikae) The third-longest stem in an *ikebana* arrangement

Taiyaki Fish-shaped sweet cake

Tamari Wheat-free soy sauce

Tatami Woven bamboo mats

Taku (in calligraphy) The downward flick to the left

Taku (in calligraphy) The downward stroke to the right

Te-arai Handwashing

Teki (in calligraphy) An upward flick from a horizontal or vertical stroke (roku or do)

Temaki Hand roll

Temizu Handwashing ritual at a temple

Tofu Soybean curd

Tokonoma Alcove

Toro Traditional Japanese lantern

Tsukemono Grilled vegetables

Tsundoku Accumulating books that won't be read

Tsuyu Sauce

Ugai Gargling

Umeboshi Pickled plums

Uramaki Inside-out roll

Usucha Thin tea

Usukuchi Light soy sauce

Utsuwa Vase

Uwabaki Indoor shoes

Wa Harmony

Wabi-sabi The beauty of change, acceptance of transience and imperfection

Wagashi Traditional Japanese confectionery

Wasabi Paste usually made from horseradish; a traditional accompaniment for sushi

Washi Mulberry paper

Washitsu Japanese-style room

Yaeba A crooked smile

Yaki onigiri Grilled rice balls

Yakuza Criminal gang members

Yatta A word describing the feeling of elation at completing a task

Yobi tsugi Mending with kintsugi in a patchwork style

Yokan Red-bean jelly

Yukata A casual cotton kimono

Zabuton Floor cushions

Endnotes

[1] https://www.japantimes.co.jp/news/2017/05/17/national/science-health/continuing-streak-japan-leads-world-life-expectancy-report-says/#.Wez7TBNSzeQ

[2] https://www.ncbi.nlm.nih.gov/pubmed/19568835

[3] http://www.npr.org/sections/health-shots/2017/07/17/536676954/forest-bathing-a-retreat-to-nature-can-boost-immunity-and-mood

[4] https://www.wsj.com/articles/SB10001424052748704631504575531932754922518

[5] http://time.com/4267661/japanese-food-healthy-diet-longevity/